The Long Walk

THE FORCED NAVAJO EXILE

The Long Walk

THE FORCED NAVAJO EXILE

JENNIFER DENETDALE
Associate Professor of History
University of New Mexico

SERIES EDITOR: PAUL C. ROSIER
Assistant Professor of History
Villanova University

CHELSEA HOUSE
PUBLISHERS
An imprint of Infobase Publishing

Cover: Some of the more than 8,000 Navajos who were forced to live at Bosque Bedondo are pictured in this 1864 photograph.

THE LONG WALK: The Forced Navajo Exile

Chelsea House
An imprint of Infobase Publishing
132 West 31st Street
New York NY 10001

Library of Congress Cataloging-in-Publication Data
Denetdale, Jennifer.
  The Long Walk : the forced Navajo exile / Jennifer Denetdale.
    p. cm. — (Landmark events in Native American History)
  Includes bibliographical references and index.
  ISBN-13: 978-0-7910-9344-3 (hardcover)
  ISBN-10: 0-7910-9344-1 (hardcover)
  1. Navajo Long Walk, 1863-1867—Juvenile literature. 2. Bosque Redondo Indian Reservation (N.M.)—Juvenile literature. 3. Navajo Indians—Relocation—Juvenile literature. 4. Navajo Indians—Government relations—Juvenile literature. I. Title. II. Series.
  E99.N3D367 2007
  978.9004'97267—dc22   2007021723

Chelsea House books are available at special discounts when purchased in bulk quantities for businesses, associations, institutions, or sales promotions. Please call our Special Sales Department in New York at (212) 967-8800 or (800) 322-8755.

You can find Chelsea House on the World Wide Web at
http://www.chelseahouse.com

Series design by Erika K. Arroyo
Cover design by Ben Peterson
Illustrations by Sholto Ainslie

Printed in the United States of America

BANG NMSG 10 9 8 7 6 5 4 3 2 1

This book is printed on acid-free paper.

All links and Web addresses were checked and verified to be correct at the time of publication. Because of the dynamic nature of the Web, some addresses and links may have changed since publication and may no longer be valid.

Contents

Who are the Diné?

IT IS ONE OF THOSE HOT SUMMER DAYS WHEN THE gathering dark clouds promise rain but are still too far away to tell if rain will fall. In Window Rock, Arizona, the capital of the Navajo Nation, Diné Tribal Council delegates dressed in a combination of Western and Navajo style clothing begin to fill the chambers for the summer legislative session. (*Diné* means the People and is the word Navajos call themselves.)[1] The Diné also call themselves *Náhokah Diné* (Earth Surface People) and *Bilá 'ashdla'* (Five-Fingered Ones). At the Navajo Nation museum and library, the staff prepare for the day's patrons, which will include Diné children who come to use the computers and to read books. Visitors from throughout the world come to the museum and visitor's center to learn about Diné culture and traditions. After visiting the museum, they might go to the tribal council chambers and Veterans Memorial Park, near the president's office. Across from a group of stores, at the main thoroughfare, the government of the Navajo Nation has created an area where Diné can sell their arts and crafts in a clean and comfortable space. Each morning, men and women set up their stands for a day of selling. Here, it is possible to buy a lunch of roasted mutton, grilled green chilies, and a hot flour tortilla. In one corner, a man and his wife place a five-gallon container of steaming blue corn mush on a small table while another woman sets boxes of Avon products next to her home-baked treats. An herbalist sits in front of rows of packaged traditional herbs. Soon, throngs of Diné will finger through the packages, in search of cures for such ailments as arthritis, acne, and headaches.

Window Rock, Arizona, is one of several Diné communities that took on an urban look beginning in the 1950s, when the tribal government began to expand. Because the tribal government is one of the largest employers in the region, many people have moved closer to Window Rock for their jobs. While many Diné have moved into urban areas like Window Rock, Tuba City, Crownpoint, or Shiprock, many still reside on the lands their family has lived on since before 1868.

THE NAVAJO HOMELAND

Diné Bikéyah, or Dinétah, as Navajos call their homeland, is a destination for many visitors. Driving across the vast expanse of the Navajo Nation—17.3 million acres that stretches across Arizona, New Mexico, and Utah—these visitors will see homes clustered together, where two or three generations live together as extended families. Western-style houses are typical, but each residence often includes a hogan—a traditional Diné home. On Dinétah, most homes face east to meet the rising sun and receive their blessings from the Holy People. Although fewer and fewer families keep livestock, herds of goats and sheep can still be seen moving among sparse brush. Motorists must watch out for the lone goat or sheep that has found its way onto the highway.

According to the 2000 U.S. census, the Navajo population was 298,200, with at least half living outside the Navajo

After the U.S. government forced the Navajo to reduce the numbers of their livestock during the 1930s and '40s, some Navajos were forced to find work outside the reservation. Here, two Navajo men from Crownpoint, New Mexico, work on a train track in 1950.

reservation at any given time.[2] Like other Native Americans, the Diné have been shaped by federal Indian policies such as termination and relocation. First, after the Federal livestock reduction program of the 1930s and 1940s, Navajos were forced to seek jobs outside of their homeland, many of whom chose to work in the railroad and agricultural industries. Second, in the 1950s, the federal government attempted to acculturate Native Americans by promising them better lives in cities such as Los Angeles, San Francisco, and Chicago. Many Navajos took the offer and moved, with the hope of finding a good job, decent housing, and better education for their children. Today, in addition to those who still look for employment outside Dinétah, Navajos whose parents or grandparents were relocated to cities often still live and work in cities. However, like their parents and grandparents, many return to Dinétah on weekends and holidays. They have retained strong ties to their Navajo culture, and in addition to visiting their relatives, they also preserve their culture by cooking traditional foods and listening to Diné stories and songs.

Today, the Navajo Nation maintains its own legislative, executive, and judicial branches of government and its own police force. In the spring of 1969, the Navajos opened the first tribal college in the United States, Navajo Community College, which was later renamed Diné College. The tribal newsletter, the *Navajo Times*, was first published in 1958 and has evolved into an independent weekly newspaper that remains the major media outlet for disseminating tribal news. Seeking self-determination, Navajo leaders have attempted to gain control of their natural resources, such as water, coal, and natural gas. One business venture is Navajo Agricultural Products Industry (NAPI), a large-scale farming operation, which, in 2006, agreed to supply Cuba with such crops as wheat, apples, yellow corn, onions, and pinto beans. The company is the first in New Mexico to sign a trade deal with Cuba. The Navajo Nation is also working to build additional grocery stories, restaurants, and hotels in Dinétah.

In the twenty-first century, it might appear that the Diné are no different than other modern Americans who drive to work in their cars, shop at malls for the latest fashions, grab a quick lunch with co-workers at a local fast food restaurant, or, after work, change into Nike sportswear and go for a jog. On the other hand, Navajos struggle with high rates of poverty and unemployment, with all of its accompanying ills such as disease, domestic violence, and homicides. In many ways, the Diné have become accustomed to American culture, for they are just as proud as others to be Americans. Nevertheless, Navajos remain mindful of how their ancestors have left them a powerful legacy, a determination to remain a sovereign people who have land, a still vital language, and a strong cultural identity.

IN THE BEGINNING

Like other people throughout the world, the Diné have stories about their origins and how they came to live in their present homeland in what is now the American Southwest. Today, Navajo parents and educators are reviving the storytelling tradition and passing on the stories of their ancestors. Many years ago, on a winter evening, a young boy and girl might have sat with an elder and listened to stories around a fire until it burned down to glowing embers. These narratives served as the foundation for their lives.

The origin of the Diné begins in the First World, which was dark. First Man and First Woman lived in this world. Spirit beings who were insect-like in appearance, with snout-like noses and claw-like hands, inhabited this world. Here, these beings committed transgressions and were forced to leave. They journeyed to the next world, which was blue. While they set about establishing themselves, once again some of their members committed a wrong. They were ordered by the beings who inhabited this world to leave and so they moved onto the next world, which was yellow in color. Yet, once again, they erred. For living with them was Coyote, so well known for his mischievous behavior. It was Coyote who caused them to have to move into the next world when he stole a monster's baby by hiding it in his coat. Only when he returned the baby did the monster abandon his pursuit of the beings. In this yellow world, they met a different people whose hair was cut straight across the forehead and who hospitably shared their food, corn. Having taken advantage of the new people they had met, they were told to move on because they were not hospitable, and therefore not welcome. They journeyed on to the next world, which was glittering or bright, and emerged into the present world, in which the Diné currently live.

Eventually, they learned from the error of their ways. During their journey through the worlds, they had also brought the soil from the mountains, which upon entering the glittering world, they set as the boundaries for their homeland. The four sacred mountains that mark Dinétah are Sisnaajiní, or Blanca Peak, in the east; Tso' dziil, or Mount Taylor, in the south; Dook'o'osłííd, or the San Francisco Peaks, in the west; and Dibé nitsah, or Mount Hesperus, in the north. The soil brought from the world below also formed two other mountains: Dził ná'oodiłii, or Huerfano Mountain—east of the center—and Ch'ool'í'í, or Gobernador Knob—the center.

It is in the Glittering World—the present world—that the beings evolved into their present human shape, which is that of the Holy People. In the Glittering World, the world as we know it today was shaped. One day First Man was out and about and heard an infant crying. Investigating, he came upon a baby girl, whom he took home to his wife, First Woman. They adopted the baby and were so pleased with her that they arranged a ceremony to celebrate her birth and to ensure her well-being and prosperity. The Holy People came and brought their songs and prayers, which are the foundation for the Blessingway ceremony. The Blessingway embodies all that is significant in Navajo life and is manifested in the concept of *Hózhó*. According to Hózhó, Navajos continually seek good health, peace, and prosperity throughout their lives and with their kin relations. Today, the Blessingway continues to be performed to ensure a person's harmony, well-being, and balance.

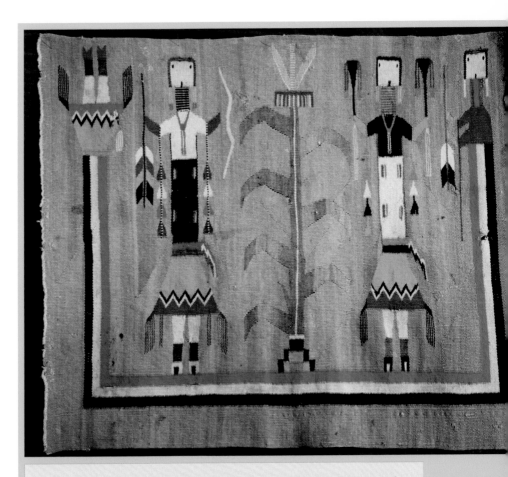

The Holy People provided the Navajos with prayers and songs and also gave them faith and courage to persevere during difficult times. Here, two Holy People flank a stalk of maize, which was their gift to the Navajo people, on this nineteenth-century blanket.

Changing Woman and Her Twin Sons

Under the loving care of First Man and First Woman, the infant who would become Asdzáá Nádleehí, or Changing Woman, thrived. Soon—some people say four days and some say four years—she grew into a young woman. Her passage into womanhood was celebrated with a ceremony, called the Kinaaldá, a puberty rite, which is still performed for girls who have become women. In preparation for the Blessing-way, the young woman was dressed in the finest clothes and adorned with shells and turquoise. Her hair was tied with a length of buckskin, the finest pair of moccasins were placed on her feet, and buckskin wraps were fitted around her legs. Dressed in her finery, she was also became known as White Shell Woman. The Holy People came and Haashch'éíłi'í, or Talking God, conducted the ceremony where he presented the 12 Hogan songs. The Holy People prayed that Asdzáá Nádleehí would be a fine mother and grandmother. She would head a fine household with plenty of good food to eat and own a sturdy hogan and flocks of horses, sheep, and goats that would sustain her and her children. They prayed that she would take care of the land and always acknowledge its sacredness and respect the animals and natural elements such as the wind, water, and fire that were also a part of the Diné world.

Changing Woman became the mother of the most famous twin sons—Naayéé Neezghári, or Monster Slayer and Tó Bájísh Chíní, or Born for Water. Their father was Jóhonaa'éí, the Sun. Like other boys, they loved to play while their mother attended to her chores and daily business. Changing Woman also worried about her sons because at this time monsters roamed the land, eating children and drinking all of the water. The people were suffering because of the monsters. One day, the boys asked their mother, "Who is our father?" She did not want to tell them but eventually relented, whereupon the twin boys immediately readied for a journey in search of their father, the Sun. However, when they found Jóhonaa'éí, they realized that he did not really know if they were indeed his sons. To prove that they were his sons, the Sun sent them on several excursions. These excursions were really tests and could have resulted in their deaths if they had failed.

Fortunately, they successfully passed all of the obstacles they faced. Their success was largely due to the help they received from Grandmother Spider and natural elements such as the wind. After they had successfully overcome the obstacles, the Sun presented gifts to them: armors of flint and arrows of lightening. The Sun also gave them horses.

With these warriors' implements, the Hero Twins returned to their mother and came to the aid of the people who were being killed by the monsters. In one still very famous case, Monster Slayer came across a monster near present-day Grants, New Mexico, who was killing people and drinking all of the available water. Monster Slayer killed the monster and then cut off his head. To make sure that the monster would not come back to life, Monster Slayer made a deep cut in the ground so that the monster's blood would move away from his body. Today, Navajos remember the story as they pass the blood that has dried into rocks just outside of Grants, New Mexico. The story reminds them that warriors are brave and protect the people from harm.

Just as the story of the Hero Twins tells about the importance of warriors, the stories of Changing Woman illustrates to young people the importance of women as mothers and grandmothers. Changing Woman was born to bring harmony and order to the world. With the birth of her sons, the world was soon rid of the dreaded monsters. Her story is one of generosity and compassion, for Changing Woman is all good and benevolent. The stories of Changing Woman and the Hero Twins are just some of the many stories Diné children hear. And while the setting may have changed from winter evenings in front of a cozy fire to one where the children might be sitting around a kitchen table, the stories convey beliefs and values that are timeless.

These stories from the creation to the establishment of the Diné in Dinétah have been the cornerstone of Navajo families and clans. They have within them the prayers and stories about how to live a harmonious life, how to prosper and be healthy, how to raise children properly, how to treat illnesses, how to establish a political community, and how to sustain one's family through livestock raising and agriculture. The stories also tell the Diné what can happen if they transgress codes of conduct and behavior; and they can tell them how to protect themselves from enemies and how to purify themselves after going into battle. Finally, the stories tell them how to treat the world and the animals around them, many of whom helped them to survive during the journey through the worlds.

EXPANDING DINÉTAH

Navajos' stories of their own history, their origins, and how they became a pastoral people whose wealth lay in their vast herds of sheep, goats, and horses, and especially in the textiles woven by the women, differs significantly from those of non-Navajo archaeologists and anthropologists who have traced Athapaskan migration from the north into the American Southwest, most likely just prior to the appearance of the Spaniards in the sixteenth century. While Diné acknowledge relatives in the north, including the Hupas of northern California, their focus is on the ways their ancestors emerged into the Glittering World and moved about with the intention of living by the Holy People's instructions.

According to Navajo beliefs, the early Diné lived in Dinétah—a region in northwestern New Mexico—among the inhabitants of Chaco Canyon and Mesa Verde. According to Diné stories, their ancestors had been a simple people who relied on tools such as digging sticks to plant their fields of corn and squash, gathered wild plants for food, and relied on bows and arrows to hunt deer. As anthropologist Klara Kelley and Navajo scholar Harris Francis have noted, Navajo narratives feature elements such as turquoise, obsidian, and shell, which were not available in the region the Navajos inhabited in the fifteenth and sixteenth centuries.[3] Just as widespread trading networks existed, in which the Diné forebears probably took active roles, they also related with the Puebloan peoples along a continuum that moved from kinship and peace to hostility. While the Diné note that some of their ceremonial knowledge came from interaction with the Puebloan people who lived nearby, they also note that their chief ceremony, the Blessingway, is distinctly Diné, because it was the Holy People who provided them with the prayers and songs.

Spanish Incursions

The Spaniards initially entered the southwest in the mid-sixteenth century, but did not establish settlements until the end of the century. Claiming the land in the name of the Spanish Crown and the indigenous peoples as vassals of Spain, the Spanish colonists established their settlements in the most fertile areas around the Rio Grande, which was often where Pueblo villages were situated. Establishing missions in order to Christianize the Pueblos, the colonists also took all available Pueblo resources, including food and labor. Not content just to indoctrinate the Pueblos and take possession of their lands and resources, the Spaniards also attempted to do the same to the Diné. Because they were largely unsuccessful in these endeavors, they conducted slave raids into Navajo country.

Although few Spaniards actually ever saw the Diné, who stayed close to their well-protected citadels, mesas, and mountainous regions, the Spanish presence, and especially the material culture and animals they brought to the New World, dramatically transformed the Diné. The first Spanish references to the Diné occurred in 1626, when Fray Geronimo de Zarate Salmeron wrote of the Apache Indians of *Navaju*. The term has been translated as a Tewa word that means "large area of cultivated fields" and was applied to the Navajos to distinguish them from their Apache cousins who did not farm to the same extent as the Navajos.[4] Three years later, Fray Alonso de Benavides noted the Navajos' presence and thought that they should be brought under Spanish control.

In 1659, the governor of New Mexico, Bernardo Lopez de Mendizabal, continued the Spanish practices of self-enrichment at the expense of indigenous peoples by ordering raids into Navajo country for women and children, many of whom he sold in the Mexican state of Sonora. In 1675 and 1678, the Spaniards ventured into Navajo country in search of victims for their slave trade. Pueblo men joined the Spanish raiders, either because they had been coerced or because they were also being attacked by Navajos. These attacks on Navajos only served to fuel hostilities between Navajos, Spaniards, and Pueblos.

Eventually, incensed at Spanish cruelty and greed, Pueblo peoples, led by the San Juan medicine man Po'pay, rebelled in 1680, and forced the Spaniards to abandon their settlements in the north. Over a period of years, the Spaniards ventured back into present-day New Mexico, attempting to gauge native temperament to decide whether they should return. It is not known the extent to which the Navajos allied with the Pueblos, although they certainly knew of the unfolding events, especially as word of the rebellion had spread beyond the region of the Diné to the Hopis.

Finally, in 1692, the Spaniards, under Diego de Vargas, returned to reestablish their colonies. Fearing reprisals for the rebellion of 1680 and remembering their treatment under Spanish rule, a number of Pueblo people fled, to live among the Navajos. While they may have intended to stay with their Diné relatives until the Spaniards left, many ultimately intermarried and stayed for the duration of their lives among the Navajos. Today, the relationships that developed between the Navajos and their Pueblo allies are chiefly remembered through the creation of clans such as the Ma'ii deeshgiizhinii [Jemez], the Naasht'ezhí Diné'é [Zuni], and the Tł'ógi [Zia]. In these cases, Pueblo women married Navajo men and their children took on the matrilineal clan names from their Pueblo mothers.

The Spanish return into New Spain meant that Pueblos and Navajos would continue to suffer their assaults. Indeed, after 1705, Navajos suffered many reprisals by the Spaniards who continued their raids into Navajo country. The Spaniards enlisted Pueblo auxiliaries in their campaigns against Navajos. Just as the Spaniards created strife between Navajos and Pueblos, their policies also caused internal conflicts among the Navajos. In 1787, a band of Navajos who lived in proximity to the Spanish settlements allied themselves with the Spaniards, and later with the Mexicans, and campaigned against their own people. The move alienated their kinspeople, and thereafter this group of Diné was known as Diné Anaa'í—the Enemy Navajo. Today, their descendants inhabit the community of To'hajiili (formerly known as Canoncito) outside of Albuquerque, New Mexico. To'hajiili is one of the 110 chapters that make up the Navajo Nation's communities.

One of the best-known campaigns, of which Navajos still tell stories, is Antonio Narbona's military operation into the Navajo stronghold, the Tséyi' (Canyon de Chelly) in 1805. As Narbona's party passed below a cave in which Diné women, children, and elders were concealed, an elderly woman who had been taken captive by the Spaniards and had managed to escape, became so incensed at the sight of the soldiers that she began shouting invectives, thereby disclosing their location. The Spanish soldiers fired hundreds of rounds into the cave, killing more than a hundred of the Diné. In addition to the Diné that they killed, the Spanish also took 33 captives. At the time, the Spanish threat was coupled with Ute and Comanche pressures from the northwest of Dinétah.

Canyon de Chelly, or Tséyi', as it is known to the Navajos, is one of the longest continually occupied areas in the United States. Located in northeastern Arizona, Tséyi' has traditionally been a Navajo stronghold, where they would go in times of danger.

A Pastoral People

The introduction of horses, sheep, and goats turned the Diné into a pastoral people. Mounted Navajo warriors ably protected their people from the enemy. At the same time, they expanded their territory, both in response to enemy pressure and the need for more grazing lands. Their sheep became one of their most prized possessions, so that even today, Navajos note that sheep can teach one how to live properly. Spanish accounts have also noted the prominence of a textile industry carried out by Navajo women. Used as blankets and clothing, these textiles became so valuable that only persons of wealth could afford them, hence the textiles came to be known as "chief's blanket," meaning that the person wearing the textile was a person of status. As anthropologist David Brugge has observed, much of what we characterize as Diné cultural practices and traits today largely evolved during this period of Navajo history.[5]

By the end of the eighteenth century, Navajos had moved their herds south into the region around Mount Taylor, which the Spaniards named Cebolleta, and then into Tséyi', to the west. Tséyi would become the Navajo stronghold in the nineteenth century. The Diné led a pastoral life, following their flocks of sheep. Extended families centered on matrilineal clanships in which women presided over their households, controlled the livestock, and dictated land use. Families set up households near water sources, where they found fertile ground for their corn and squash. As summer approached, family members moved sheep and goats into the mountainous regions, such as the Chuska mountain ranges, where there was plentiful grass and water. Others stayed behind to keep a watchful eye on the cornfields. In the fall, they moved down from the mountains. The seasonal pattern of moving with the flocks from the flat lands to the mountains was constantly interrupted by foreigners who often came into Dinétah looking for wealth in the form of gold and silver, for land to cultivate, and for slaves. While historians have noted periods of peace between Spaniards and Navajos, there was almost unremitting hostilities between them that continued into the Mexican period, from 1820 to 1848, when Americans claimed the Southwest.

American Expansion and Navajo Resistance

FROM THE SPANISH TO THE AMERICAN PERIOD—THE eighteenth to the middle of the nineteenth century—a local economy based on limited farming and sheep herding evolved. Farming and sheep herding were important to both New Mexicans and indigenous peoples alike; however, the slave trade was crucial to the economy of the region and a factor in the hostilities between Navajos, Pueblos, and New Mexicans. While many of the conflicts between indigenous peoples and whites resulted from native challenges to white claims to land, the Navajo experience was also distinguished by their objections to the slave raids into their country. As historian James Brooks revealed in his study of captivity in the Southwest, from 1800 to 1860, a pattern of violence, occasional formal campaigns, and short-lived peace treaties between newly installed governments and Navajos occurred during this period.[6]

In 1845, American journalist John O'Sullivan coined the term *manifest destiny* to describe white expansion westward.

According to this doctrine, white Americans were destined to spread from the eastern part of the United States to the Pacific coast by the will of God. White Americans had long been moving westward before O'Sullivan's declaration; for the prospects of free land drew eager whites toward California and into the southwest. As early as the 1820s, American traders and trappers made positive reports of the Diné and often expressed admiration and sympathy for their efforts to resist the Mexicans living in present-day New Mexico. For example, frontiersman Josiah Gregg believed that the New Mexicans and their governor had "greatly embittered the disposition of the neighboring savages, especially the Navajos, by repeated acts of cruelty and ill-faith well calculated to provoke hostilities."[7] It had been easy for the Americans to champion the Navajo cause against the Mexicans when they had little involvement with the Navajos, but once they assumed power, their favorable reports quickly turned negative, especially because the Navajos did not welcome any group that invaded their country. Although Navajos had good reason to defend their territory, family, and kin, the Americans placed the blame for the cycles of hostilities that frequently occurred in the southwest squarely upon the Navajos and the Apaches.

Americans saw the Navajos and Apaches as their enemies, particularly because the groups did not recognize any difference among the waves of conquerors who had entered their homeland and attempted to subjugate them. The U.S. takeover of Mexico's northern territories began in 1846 with the arrival of Colonel Stephen Kearny's Army of the West from Fort Leavenworth, Kansas. Beleaguered by continual Navajo attacks and retaliations, Governor Manuel Armijo could only look on as U.S. forces marched toward the capital of Santa Fe. Historian Frank McNitt compared the American takeover to the storm before the calm. He wrote, "like

At the beginning of the Mexican-American War in 1846, Stephen W. Kearny led a contingent of U.S. troops to present-day Santa Fe, New Mexico, where he drove out Mexican forces and established a civilian government. Shortly after he arrived, Kearny sent Colonel Alexander Doniphan to meet with Navajo leaders to establish the first treaty between the United States and the Navajos.

thunderheads moving before curtains of rain, the sweeping shadow of these forces moved down the Mora Valley in the form of a marching army of fifteen hundred men."[8] Such imagery strongly suggests that the land, like the people, was sorely in need of relief from a drought. Just as thunder with its accompanying life-giving water can revive the earth and all living things, so too did the Americans bring new life to the southwest, reviving the land and the people. While the Americans might have seen themselves as a liberating force, the Navajos certainly disagreed. They would take the necessary measure to protect themselves against intruders and defend their rights to live in a manner they saw fit.

Upon his arrival in Santa Fe, Colonel Kearny announced to the residents that he had come as a caretaker, not as a conqueror, "to protect the persons and property of all quiet and peaceable inhabitants . . . against their enemies, the Eutaws, the Navajos, and others."[9] Almost immediately, the Americans recognized that they would face resistance from the Navajos. While the Americans might have announced their claim to the southwest, Navajo leaders did not immediately acknowledge them. Neither did they visit Santa Fe to meet the U.S. officials. Rather, based on reports of continued clashes between New Mexicans and Navajos, in 1846, Kearny ordered Colonel Alexander Doniphan into Navajo country to ascertain whether the Navajos were willing to accept American rule. Doniphan's meeting with Navajo leaders was the first in a series of councils that resulted in a treaty between the two groups.

THE FIRST TREATY BETWEEN THE NAVAJOS AND U.S. GOVERNMENT

At Ojo Del Oso, or Shush Bitó (Bear Spring), as the Navajos knew the place, Doniphan asserted to the assembled Navajo leaders that the United States claimed New Mexico by right of conquest and that they would protect all of its new citizens, including the Diné. He addressed the ongoing war between

New Mexicans and Navajos and emphasized to the Diné leaders that their attacks on New Mexicans must cease or they would face war with the United States. On behalf of the Navajo contingent, the respected headman Zarcillas Largos answered the Americans with the eloquent and powerful oratory for which Diné leaders were known. The Diné had been waging war against the New Mexicans for years; the New Mexicans had plundered their villages, killed their people, and captured many prisoners. Zarcillas Largos noted that his people had just cause for their war against the New Mexicans, for they had lost many of their women and children to the slave trade. He continued his speech to the Americans, saying, "You have lately commenced a war against the same people. You are powerful. You have great guns and many brave soldiers. You have therefore conquered them, the very thing we have been attempting to do for so many years." However, he also chastised the Americans, "You now turn upon us for attempting to do what you done yourselves. We cannot see why you have cause of quarrel with us for fighting the New Mexicans on the west, while you do the same thing on the east."[10] He ended his declarations with an entreaty: The Americans should allow the Diné to settle their disputes with the New Mexicans.

Largos's speech attests to Navajo perceptions of their own place in the southwest. In the nineteenth century, Navajo leaders believed they were equal, if not superior, to the Americans. However, Largos did acknowledge the Americans' superior firepower and raised questions about the nature of American interests in the southwest; for it was clear to the Navajos that, like the Mexicans, the Americans were determined to claim the region at whatever cost it took. The Diné saw the Americans neutralize the Mexicans, something they had attempted to do for more than a two decades. Nevertheless, on November 22, 1846, the first of nine treaties was agreed upon between the Americans and the Navajo leaders. The treaty called for a lasting peace between the two

One of the signatories of the first treaty between the United States and the Navajos was Manuelito. Known by several names in Navajo, including *Hastin Ch'il Hajin* (Man of Black Weeds), Manuelito resisted American incursion into Dinétah, the Navajo homeland.

parties, mutual trade, and the restoration of property and citizens to each side. However, the failure of the Americans to enforce the provision that Navajos would have their women

MANUELITO: CHAMPION OF NAVAJO SOVEREIGNTY

Known as *Hastin Ch'il Hajin*, or Man from Black Weeds, Manuelito (c. 1818–1894) was born into the *Bit'ahni* clan (Folded Arms People) near Bear Ears, Utah, around 1818. Noted for his resistance to Mexican and American invasions of Dinétah, Manuelito is revered by his people for his belief in Navajo sovereignty and his avocation of a Western education for Navajo children so that they might be able to better protect their people.

Navajo stories say that when Manuelito's father learned of his son's birth, he took the infant and presented him to the Holy People and prophesied that his son would be a great leader and warrior of his people. Following the teachings set down for warriors, Manuelito became a revered leader. Manuelito's marriage to the daughter of the headman Narbona provided him with the wise leader's insight. In later years, Manuelito married another woman known to Americans as Juanita. As he traveled throughout Diné Bikéyah, he often took this wife with him. In her, he found a valuable companion whose counsel he often sought.

Today, Navajos remember Manuelito's devotion to his people. He was appointed head of the first Navajo police force that kept order on the reservation. In 1874, he traveled with his wife and other Navajo leaders to Washington, D.C., to meet President Grant. In the 1880s, he sent two of his sons to Carlisle Indian School in Carlisle, Pennsylvania, as a message to his people that they should not fear Western education for their children. In 1894, Manuelito died from a combination of diseases, including alcoholism. His widow Juanita and his daughters carried on his messages about the importance of education for the children and the retention of land for the coming generations. Today, Manuelito remains a popular role model for Navajos who have composed songs and poetry about their leader.

and children returned to them would remain a point of contention over the coming years.

One of the signatories of the treaty was Manuelito, the son-in-law of the revered leader Narbona. Known to the Diné by several names, including `Ashkii Diyinii (Holy Boy), *Noobaahi Jótá* (Warrior Grabbed Enemy), *N'aabeáána badaai* (son-in-law of late Texan), and *Hastin Ch'il Hajin* (Man of Black Weeds), he was best known to non-Indians as Manuelito. Nabana Badane meant that he was the son-in-law of Narbona. At 28 years of age, Manuelito was young for a *naa't́aani* (leader). According to oral tradition, at the news of his birth, Manuelito's father had come, taken the newborn into the sunlight, and presented him to the Holy People. He prophesized that his son would be a great warrior whose skills would protect his people and that his words would be taken to heart. Manuelito was accustomed to being around leaders in his early life. His father, Cayetano, who resided around Bear Ears, in present-day southern Utah, had strongly resisted foreign rule. Manuelito's brother Cayetanito, one of the leaders to visit Washington, D.C., in 1874, was a prominent figure in the Mount Taylor area. Two of his other brothers, *K'ayelli* (One with Quiver) and El Ciego (the Blind One), also followed Manuelito's lead.

Unfortunately, the treaty of Ojo Del Oso was short lived, as conflict between the Navajos and New Mexicans began almost immediately. Between 1847 and 1849, warfare continued unabated, and Kearny's proclamation that civilians could continue their war upon the Navajos if their women, children, and livestock had been seized heightened the hostilities. Reports of Navajo depredations on New Mexican settlements poured into Santa Fe. After a second treaty was signed with the Navajos and several excursions into Navajo country failed to bring hostilities to an end, Colonel John M. Washington proceeded with plans to control the Navajos.

WASHINGTON'S EXPEDITION INTO NAVAJO TERRITORY

Taking 178 U.S. soldiers, 123 New Mexico volunteers (slave raiders), and 60 Pueblo scouts, Washington left Santa Fe for Navajo country. On August 30, 1849, the military expedition camped near Tunicha Creek, north of present-day Naschitti, New Mexico, and near Copper Pass (now known as Narbona Pass). One of the men with Washington penned his observations of being in Navajo country. After seeing their bountiful fields of corn and wheat, he noted that the Navajos were far from being "savages" like white people believed.

At this time, several Navajo leaders approached Washington's camp. Washington immediately accused them of stealing livestock and killing New Mexican citizens. The leaders responded in much the same manner as they had in earlier communications with those outsiders who invaded their country. The headmen did not have control of all of their people, and yes, there were lawless men among them, but they wanted peace and were willing to make some retribution in livestock. Washington requested that the two parties negotiate a treaty the following day and would travel to Tséyi' to formally sign the treaty.

The Navajo leaders returned the following day. Among them was the aging Narbona, who was widely known for his efforts to keep peace. The Navajo contingent also turned over some of their livestock as a sign of good faith. Then, the treaty negotiations commenced with Narbona representing the Navajos. At the end of the meeting, the Diné headman explained that he would not be at the formal treaty signing but would send two other leaders, Armijo and Pedro José, to which Washington agreed. Then the Navajo leader Antonio Sandoval began speaking. Sandoval and his people lived the closest to the New Mexican settlements and so sought compromises with the Americans in order to ensure the safety of his band. He and his people had a history of siding with

The father-in-law of Manuelito, Narbona was a prominent
Navajo leader who is well known for his decisive victory over
a much larger Mexican force at Bééshłichí'ii Bigiz (Narbona
Pass) in 1835. Despite his peaceful intentions toward the
Americans, Narbona was killed and then scalped by the
U.S. Army during treaty negotiations in 1849.

the New Mexicans and had even sold other Navajos into the slave trade. Now, he accompanied the Americans and acted as the translator for the proceedings between the two parties. For good reason he was not trusted by his fellow Navajos. Sandoval's harsh speech stirred the Navajo warriors, and tensions began to rise further when a New Mexican with the military claimed that the Navajos had one of his horses.[11]

Washington ordered the Navajos to return the horse immediately. In the face of the impending conflict, the Diné leaders tried to calm their men. While the men tried to restore order, Washington ordered his riflemen to begin firing upon the Navajos. As the soldiers fired upon the Navajos, many fought back while others fled. When the conflict subsided, Narbona lay dead from multiple wounds. The murder of Narbona, who was known for his peaceful intentions toward the Americans, was perceived as an egregious act by his people. The Navajos were further insulted when one of Washington's men scalped Narbona. As part of the Navajo delegation, the young Manuelito witnessed the death of his father-in-law. He would have to inform his wife's family, certainly not a task he relished. Narbona's death and the assault upon his people no doubt confirmed Manuelito's conviction that the Americans could not be trusted. Six other Navajos also died, while the military expedition lost only a few horses. Washington justified Narbona's murder by stating to his superiors that the head chief of the nation had been a scourge to the inhabitants of New Mexico for the last 30 years. However, as historian Frank McNitt has written, Washington's assertion about Narbona was simply untrue.[12]

FORT DEFIANCE

In the hopes of creating a lasting peace, the Navajo leaders signed what would become one of two treaties that would be ratified with the Americans on September 9, 1849. Its provisions called for the Navajos to surrender livestock taken from the settlements, ensured free passage across Navajo country for American settlers, and permitted the U.S. government to establish military and trading posts in the Navajos' homeland. The Navajo leaders' agreement to allow the establishment of forts set the stage for unremitting warfare and unimaginable suffering, particularly after Colonel Edwin Sumner established Fort Defiance in the heart of Diné territory in 1851. Over the span of several years, Navajo leaders objected to American claims to prime grazing lands surrounding the fort. In particular, Manuelito claimed the lands for his own use. This dispute eventually led to a war between the U.S. Army and the Navajos in 1858. Further, Manuelito's challenge to the Americans served as a pivotal point—the "final and fateful turning point in [white] relations with the Navajo nation,"— where an unfolding set of conflicts would result in Manuelito's bitter defeat and then his captivity at Bosque Redondo.[13]

In 1857, Major William Thomas Harbaugh Brooks assumed command at Fort Defiance. Manuelito did not immediately come to the fort to visit the new commander, making Brooks wonder about the state of their relations with the Navajos. Later, when the leader did come to the fort, Brooks described Manuelito's visit, writing to his superiors that the headman had informed him that Navajos would allow the military to graze their livestock at Ewell's hay camp, near Fort Defiance. Upon visiting the site, however, Brooks discovered that Manuelito meant to keep at least half of the lands for his own use, much to Brooks' displeasure. He also reported that Manuelito gave notice that he was resigning as the U.S. government-appointed chief and had sent a messenger with the baton and medal, signatories of office, to Brooks, which he refused. Several days later, on a day set aside to distribute farming implements to the Navajos, 300 to 400 members of the tribe arrived at the fort, including the headmen Zarcillos Largos and Hijo de Juanico. Brooks, noting that Largos did not stop to talk with him, requested reinforcements, for it seemed to him that conflict with the Diné was inevitable.

As Manuelito and his men continued to challenge the Americans at the fort for the nearby grazing fields, Navajo leaders recovered livestock and returned them to the New Mexicans. On April 5, 1858, Captain John P. Hatch encountered Manuelito and Sarcillos Largos with a large force of their warriors. Manuelito delivered 117 sheep to the captain and said that the remainder of the sheep had been killed, sold, or distributed among the Navajos. The reports from this period repeatedly note that Navajos attempted to return sheep and other livestock that other Navajos had taken, and while some Navajos were indeed raiding the New Mexican settlements, there were many others who played no part in these thefts. Hatch turned back, fearing an attack with such a large show of force by the Navajos. On May 29, Brooks's men attempted to drive out the Navajos' flocks from Ewell's camp, many of which belonged to Manuelito. Witnessing their attempts, Manuelito approached the fort with his men and addressed Brooks. He informed the major that the water, grass, and grounds outside the military post belonged to him, and that "he was born and raised there, and that he would not give it up."[14] Brooks replied that he would retain the military's use of the lands even if it meant using force. That night, his soldiers went to the field and slaughtered Manuelito's herd of cattle.

Following this slaughter, the U.S. Army kept a wary eye on Manuelito and other Diné leaders. Major Brooks noted that the day after the livestock was killed, Zarcillos Largos had come to the fort and stated that he favored peace and that Manuelito was foolish for insisting on ownership of the grazing lands. Brooks handed Manuelito's baton to Largos, indicating that it had been found in the field where the cattle had been killed. Largos shared information with Brooks about Navajo leaders sending a request to Santa Fe for reimbursement for Manuelito's livestock.

WAR BETWEEN THE NAVAJOS AND U.S. ARMY

The murder of Brooks's black slave, Jim, interpreted by many historians as a retributive act for the loss of Manuelito's cattle, served as the beginning of an all-out war between the Navajos and the U.S. Army. One day a Navajo man, reportedly from Cayentano's band, came into the fort where he attempted to sell a blanket. After a few hours inside the encampment, he suddenly took aim and shot Brook's slave. In a report he sent to his superiors, Major Brooks wrote that on July 12 a Navajo man had come into the fort and fired an arrow at Jim. The wounded Jim "never uttered a word or exclamation, but attempted to pull the arrow out, in doing which he broke it off near the head."[15] The doctor was unable to extract the head of the arrow from Jim's body, and he died four days later.

Enraged by the seeming impunity of the Navajos, Brooks insisted that the perpetrator be brought to him for justice. A southerner, Brooks believed that Jim was his property and that he should receive recompense for Jim. He also believed that the "colored" races were inferior and that he should put the Navajos in their proper place. Zarcillos Largos came into the fort after the incident and informed Brooks that he had no control over men from another band. Besides, he added, Brooks had not been in a rush to compensate Manuelito for the slaughter of his livestock. Largos agreed to look into the matter once he had returned from an errand.

To appease Brooks, the Navajos eventually brought in the body of the man whom they said had killed Jim. However, the U.S. Army surgeon's examination revealed that it was not the body of the man whom they sought. Further enraged at Navajo resistance, Brooks notified his superiors that he had given the Navajos more than adequate time to hand over the culprit, but they had refused to comply. He wrote, "Our duty remains to chastise them into obedience to our laws—After tomorrow morning war is proclaimed against them."[16]

Major Brooks's insistence that the man who killed his slave be turned over to him, coupled with reports of Navajo raids on New Mexican communities, led to a series of battles over the course of four months. The battles were costly to the Diné: At least 200 of their warriors were killed while the U.S. troops experienced far fewer fatalities. Once again, perhaps as a means to temporarily halt conflicts with the Americans, the Navajo leaders signed yet another treaty at Fort Defiance. This treaty, negotiated and signed by Colonels B. L. E. Bonneville and James L. Collins for the United States and 15 Diné leaders, including Manuelito, established an eastern boundary for the Navajos' homeland, payment of indemnification by the tribe for depredations committed by Navajos, the release of all captives by both parties involved, and waiver of the demand for the surrender of the murderer who started the war. The U.S. Army also demanded the right to send expeditions through Navajo country and to establish additional military posts. However, Congress did not ratify this treaty.

On April 30, 1860, Manuelito and fellow chief Barboncito led an attack on Fort Defiance. In the early morning, approximately 1,000 Navajo warriors stormed the fort. They were unsuccessful, largely because the three companies inside the fort had superior firepower. The attack caused New Mexicans and the U.S. Army alike to agree that it was necessary to make war on the Navajos. As one New Mexican citizen declared, it was not possible to change the Navajos: "You might as well make a hyena adopt the habits of a poodle dog,"[17] he said.

The attack on Fort Defiance renewed New Mexicans' daring, and they ventured into Navajo country to capture Navajo women and children. On one such foray, the raiders, who included Zuni auxiliaries, came across Zarcillos Largos, whom they promptly murdered. Largos's death was a great

BARBONCITO: ELOQUENT LEADER OF THE NAVAJOS

Barboncito (c. 1825–1871) was born in lower Canyon de Chelly, in present-day Arizona, around 1825, to a woman of the ma'iideesh-giizhinii (Coyote Pass or Jemez clan) and an unknown father. His warrior name was Hashke Yich'i'adehyilwod, "He Ran Down Toward the Enemy in Anger." Like other Diné or Navajo headmen, he was well versed in ceremonies such as the Blessingway and Enemyway. He is perhaps best known by the name given to him by the Mexicans, "Barboncito." There are references to other Navajo leaders with similar names, including Barbon and El Barbon, making it uncertain about the identity of some leaders. However, by the 1850s, Barboncito had become a prominent headman. Today, Navajos remember their leader as a man who used his knowledge and skill as a warrior on behalf of his people, because his power for oratory was a significant factor in the Americans' decision to allow the Navajo people to return to their homeland in 1868. After the Navajos returned to their homeland, Barboncito remained an important leader recognized by both Navajos and U.S. officials. Because the Navajo population was always too large for their reservation, they soon spilled into regions designated as public domain. Their use of these lands for grazing was contested by white settlers, including Mormons who lived on the northwestern boundaries of Dinétah. Sometimes during these disputes both Navajos and whites were killed. Barboncito worked to quell the disturbances and to keep the peace between Navajos and whites. Today, Barboncito is remembered as an important peace leader of the Navajos, and when war was inevitable, he proved courageous and faithful. His eloquence and conviction served the purpose of bringing the People back to their sacred homeland.

loss for the Diné, for he had been greatly respected for his avocations for peace. Indeed, during a *naachid*—one of the largest political councils where the Navajos met to decide matters concerning all of their people—they gathered to hear their chiefs make cases for war or peace with the Americans. Largos had argued eloquently and persuasively for peace. He had entreated the people to listen to his message, for he had had a dream about the ruins that war would bring if they decided to fight the Americans. However, Manuelito, who favored war, had carried the day with his oratory. The people found his message compelling, and they rushed back to their residences to prepare for the inevitable conflict.

Another event that moved Navajos toward war happened on September 22, 1861, at Fort Fauntleroy, which was established near present-day Fort Wingate in northwestern New Mexico. As part of a campaign to gain Navajo trust, the commander, Thomas T. Fauntleroy, distributed rations. The distribution days were festive and Navajos and whites alike betted on horse races and card games. On one of these occasions, more than 300 Navajos gathered at Fauntleroy in anticipation of a peace council. As was typical, horse races were scheduled. For several days, the soldiers successfully betted on their favorite horse, which was owned by the post's assistant surgeon. On September 22, Manuelito brought his horse to race. During the course of the race, Manuelito's horse left the track, and it was discovered that its bridle had been cut. The Navajos demanded another race but the soldiers refused. When the Navajos protested, the soldiers opened fire on the crowd of Navajo men, women, and children.

A PLAN FOR REMOVAL

With the start of the Civil War in 1861, many U.S. troops stationed at forts in the southwest headed east to take part in the conflict. However, a new policy had gained support in this region of the country. Originally implemented in 1830, the Indian Removal Act paved the way for white settlement east of the Mississippi River. However, by the 1860s, Americans wanted more land, including the Navajo homeland. One of the primary advocates of this policy was General Edward R. S. Canby, who favored Navajo removal from their homeland but was consumed with the Civil War and so left its implementation to James Carleton who took command upon Canby's departure in May 1861. Paramount to Brigadier General Carleton's interest in removing the Navajos was reports of gold. Writing a letter to another soldier stationed at the Walker mines in Arizona, Carleton requested his presence so that he could lead a military unit into Navajo country.

In addition to the Navajos, Carleton's removal plan included the Mescalero Apaches, who were also seen as a threat to continued white settlement in the region. Considering several areas to establish a reservation, he finally settled on a place adjacent to Fort Sumner in the northeastern part of New Mexico. Ignoring reports that it was uninhabitable—the water was alkaline, wood was scarce, and the summers and winters were harsh—Carleton outlined his plan. At Bosque Redondo—a million-acre reservation established expressly for the Navajos and Mescalero Apaches at Fort Sumner in southeastern New Mexico—Navajos and Mescaleros would be grouped into villages and learn the arts of civilization. They would become farmers, be instructed in Christian virtues, and their children would be educated in white American ways. Carleton declared to his superiors that in order to bring Navajos under control it was necessary to use force, for they could "no more be trusted than you can trust the wolves that run through their mountains." If the U.S. Army placed them on a reserve far "from the haunts and hills and hiding places of their country, and there be kind to them," they would "acquire new habits, new ideas, new modes of life." Carleton went on to note that it was impossible to retrain the older Indians, but possibilities for their "civilization" lay with the children: "the young ones will take their places without these longings: and thus, little by little, they will become a happy and contented people."[18] By September 1863, Carleton stated his plan: All captives who surrendered voluntarily would go to Bosque Redondo. All male Navajos who resisted would be shot. Those who surrendered would be given food, clothing, and shelter and then should await orders to be moved to Bosque Redondo.

REDSHIRT PURSUES THE NAVAJOS

To force the Navajos' surrender and relocate them to the reservation, Carleton enlisted the renowned Indian fighter Kit Carson to convey his message: "Go to the Bosque Redondo, or we will pursue and destroy you. We will not make peace with you on any other terms."[19] Carson was known by many native peoples, for he had not only served as a guide for whites coming west but also as an Indian agent in the service of the federal government. Prior to Carson's campaign, the U.S. Army had been unsuccessful in its attempt to force the Navajos to surrender. Not only did the Navajos know their country so well that they could call upon the Holy People and the natural world for protection, but Tséyi', with its high canyon walls proved to be an impenetrable fortress. Inside the canyon there was Spider Rock, a towering needle-like rock formation, which served as a haven. Once the Diné had climbed up its steep sides on yucca ladders and then pulled up the ladders, it was impossible to reach them.

In the summer of 1863, Carson began his campaign against the Navajos. Moving with 221 men from Los Lunas to Fort Wingate, he added an additional 326 men to his command. Carson fed his soldiers and livestock on Navajo wheat and corn and then destroyed the rest of the crops. Every hogan he and his men encountered was destroyed. Livestock was slaughtered and their carcasses left to rot. The peach trees lining the canyon floors were slashed. Such actions

The Navajos often used Spider Rock, which lies within the confines of Canyon de Chelly, as a place of sanctuary. The Navajos would climb up the needle-like rock formation on yucca ladders and then pull them up before their pursuers could capture them.

were a key part of his plan to defeat the Navajos. In his first attempts to force the Navajos to surrender, however, Carson was unsuccessful. He indiscriminately targeted women and children and allowed volunteers to take captives as payment. Carson's men also humiliated and murdered Navajos who surrendered. By the fall of 1863, Carson had yet to engage the Navajos in open conflict; rather, a group of Diné warriors followed the militia, taking livestock and attacking the army's horses, while continually embarrassing Carson's men. As a result of the abuse they suffered and because stories that circulated told of their people being murdered, many Navajos refused to surrender. As historian Clifford Trazfer noted, Navajos were convinced that Carson's campaign was a war of extermination: "The Indians felt that they had no choice but to remain fast in their mountains and to avoid the onslaught of the troops, who they feared would murder them if they surrendered."[20]

After months of little success, and with winter approaching, Carleton ordered Carson to continue the war against the Navajos with an invasion of the Navajo stronghold, Tsé yí. Navajos recall this time in their history as the "fearing time," when their people were constantly on the run from the soldiers. In the 1960s and '70s, Navajo elders recalled stories of their grandmothers and grandfathers who had faced the soldiers and the New Mexican volunteers. It seemed to the Navajos that all of their enemies, including the Utes, Zunis, and other Pueblo peoples, had been unleashed on them. Chahadineli Benally, a medicine man who was approximately 85 years old in the 1970s, shared his story of how his great-grandmother had been captured by New Mexicans. Taken captive, the girl was brought into a Mexican household, where she found sympathy from a Mexican woman who eventually helped the girl escape. Eli Gorman said that Carson, who was known to the Navajos as *Bi'éé Łichíí'í*, which translates to Red Shirt, kept the Diné on the run.[21] The Indian fighter, who was also known as "Rope Thrower," indiscriminately captured hostile *and* peaceful Diné. Many men and women were killed, and children were sold into slavery. If they surrendered, many were ashamed of the state they were in. Some came in with hardly a stitch of clothing, and the soldiers only gave them a piece of cloth to cover their bodies. Carson's forays into the stronghold proved too much for the Diné, who had been severely weakened by his scorch-and-burn tactics.

THE NAVAJOS SURRENDER

By late 1863, thousands of Navajos, destitute and starving, had surrendered at the U.S. forts. One of the first head-men to capitulate, Delgadito and 187 of his people came in late November 1863 and were forcibly marched to Bosque Redondo. After a brief stay, Delgadito and three other Nava-jos took Carleton's message back to Diné bikéyah: The People must surrender and move to Bosque Redondo, where they would be able to live in peace. Delgadito told all the Navajos he found that he had spoken personally to General Carleton and that the Navajos would be shown no mercy if they con-tinued to resist. Some of the leaders listened to Delgadito's message. At the end of January 1864, Delgadito arrived at Fort Wingate with 680 Navajos.

In March 1864, General Carleton reported to his com-mander that more than 3,000 Navajos had surrendered at Fort Defiance and would join the other prisoners at Bosque Redondo, bringing the total number of Navajo captives to 6,000. The campaign was winding down; however, the attacks against Navajos did not cease as slave raiders found it profit-able to continue their raids. Some of the most distinguished of the Navajo leaders surrendered at the forts, including Her-rera Grande. Throughout the spring of 1864, Navajos had much to fear from the raiders who attacked the Diné in their homeland and stole their children along the route to Bosque Redondo. Carleton made a few attempts to return captives

After leading the First California Infantry in an overland campaign from California to Texas during the Civil War, Brigadier General James Carleton was appointed commander of the Department of New Mexico in 1862. Over the next few years, Carleton led an ongoing campaign against the Indians of the southwest, including the Navajo.

to their Navajo families but found it difficult because captors refused to relinquish their stolen property.

Although the military was finding it impossible to care for its Diné prisoners, Carleton was still eager to force Manuelito and Barboncito to surrender. The *Santa Fe Gazette* published an officer's report about the need to capture or kill Manuelito, who was so influential that his capture or death could mean that the Navajos would surrender. In early August 1864, soldiers surprised Barboncito and his people who were in Canyon de Chelly. The leader surrendered with the remainder of his kin, who numbered only five men, a woman, and a child. Although he made the journey to the prison camp, he left within the year with a group of his people and lived among Apache allies in their mountains. However, the Diné leader would surrender again and returned to Fort Sumner in November 1866.

In the spring of 1864, military officers received word that Manuelito would turn himself in. Manuelito arrived at Fort Defiance but refused to go to Bosque Redondo. An officer informed the Diné leader that he had but one choice and that was to go to Bosque Redondo. Learning about the living conditions at the reservation, Manuelito requested a visit from Herrera, one of the chiefs at the internment camp. In a report dated March 21, 1865, Carleton related the results of Herrera's meeting with Manuelito. Herrera explained that Manuelito was in poor condition, that he had about 50 people with him, and that he had few horses and sheep. Manuelito said, "Here is all I have in the world. See what a trifling amount. You see how poor they are. My children are eating roots."[22] Herrera reported that Manuelito refused to surrender and that his people should never cross the Rio Grande or go beyond the sacred mountains. He would remain in his homeland and suffer the consequences. At their kinsman's declaration, the women in his camp began to cry in distress. Throughout 1864 and into

1866, Manuelito and his band eluded the Americans and New Mexican and Ute slave raiders.

In the 1990s, Tiana Bighorse published the stories her father, Gus Bighorse, had shared with her. Bighorse's stories reveal the conditions the Navajos faced during the fearing time and indicate how leaders like Manuelito inspired their people to keep their courage. Gus's own mother and father had been murdered earlier, during the time when soldiers were combing through the Navajos' homeland. In his account, Gus was determined not to surrender, and he recalls Manuelito's urgings to be brave. The leader counseled his people, saying, "Just because they capture you and even take your life, it's just you and not all your people who will suffer." If they were caught, they should say to their enemy, "Go ahead and kill me, and I will shed my blood on my own land, not some strange land. And my people will have the land even if I die."[23]

In 1866, after thousands of his fellow Navajos had surrendered to the U.S. Army and had been forced to endure the "Long Walk," Manuelito finally admitted defeat. Wounded and ill, the great warrior led his remaining kin to Fort Wingate, where they were to await a military escort to Bosque Redondo. With him were approximately 50 of his band, which most likely included his wife Juanita and their daughters and sons. At Bosque Redondo, where more than 8,000 Navajos and several hundred Mescalero Apaches attempted to eke out a living, Manuelito remained an influential leader who looked out for the welfare of his people. It was a harsh life at the reservation. In the late 1960s, Manuelito's son-in-law Dághá Chíí Bik'is related a story he had heard from Manuelito about conditions at Bosque Redondo. He said, "Many of them [Navajos] died from starvation. The kind of food they had to eat, many died from that. Also I think a larger percent of deaths was caused from homesickness. They wept from day-to-day."[24]

The stories of the Navajo experience during American expansion into the southwest are important in the history of white American and indigenous people's relationships. Although the Diné were overpowered by the military might of the U.S. Army, and met a fate similar to other native peoples, their story is also unique in that they had ably asserted their rights to live as they wished and returned to their homeland against great odds. Their ability to overcome extreme oppression in the nineteenth century continues to give them hope that they can continue to survive as a culturally distinct people who will someday attain true sovereignty. The next phase of their experiences under American rule, their defeat, and then their forced march to Bosque Redondo remains an important part of who they are as they look forward to the future.

The Forced Relocation to New Mexico

IN THE FALL OF 1862, BRIGADIER GENERAL JAMES H. Carleton had assumed command of the U.S. Army's Department of New Mexico. He was determined to defeat the Mescalero Apaches and Navajos, because he, like many other New Mexican citizens, believed them to be the instigators of hostilities and unrest in the region. In 1862, Carleton first ordered Kit Carson to subdue the Mescalero Apaches and then the Navajos by any means possible. By March 1863, approximately 400 Mescaleros had arrived at Bosque Redondo, and Carson then turned his attention to the Navajos. With five companies of New Mexican Volunteers under his command, Carson implemented his scorch-and-burn policy in the late fall and winter of 1864. Rendered destitute and thoroughly demoralized by such brutal war tactics, thousands of Navajos surrendered at forts Wingate and Defiance from 1863 to 1867.

Although they feared Kit Carson and his men, the Navajos had few options but to leave their hideouts; for they would surely freeze to death if they did not die from starvation. Initially, small groups of 10 to 30 arrived at the forts; however,

By November 1864, at least 8,570 Navajo men, women, and children had been forced to settle at Bosque Redondo, on the Pecos River in east-central New Mexico. This map illustrates one of the main routes the Navajos were forced to take from Fort Defiance to Fort Sumner.

when Kit Carson entered Tséyi', thousands sought safety in the forts. By November 1864, U.S. military officials at Bosque Redondo reported that at least 8,570 men, women, and children had made the forced march to Bosque Redondo. It is possible that more than 11,000 Navajos were removed to Bosque Redondo, given that it is not known how many died along the trails or the number of prisoners stolen by the slave raiders who followed the forced march. Further, by 1866, captives were escaping the reservation, and U.S. officials were powerless to stop the flow returning to their homeland. Many made a second journey to Bosque Redondo after seeing the horrendous conditions in their homeland. Finally, while a majority of the Navajo people made the march to Bosque Redondo, there were others who hid in remote regions of Dinétah, in present-day northern Arizona and southern Utah.

NAVAJO NARRATIVES OF THE FEARING TIME

U.S. military reports during this period can provide some information about removal to Bosque Redondo, including population counts, the number of miles traveled on the marches, and the change in soldiers' orders; however these reports can also seem objective and aloof. Moreover, Navajo oral tradition often contradicts American written reports, which has made some doubt the veracity of Navajo accounts. Navajo narratives of the Long Walk provide accounts of their ancestors' daily experiences and their struggle to overcome almost insurmountable obstacles. Today the Diné continue to convey to the next generation the stories of their ancestors' ordeal. Navajo listeners express anger, shock, and sadness when they hear of the injustices and inhumane treatment that their ancestors received at the hands of the U.S. government and its white citizens. At the same time, they voice awe and appreciation for grandmothers and grandfathers who survived incredible odds. Had their ancestors not relied on the Holy People to give them faith and courage, the Diné might not be here today. As the Diné poet Luci Tapahonso reminds young Navajos with her story of the Long Walk, "You are here because of what happened to your great-grandmother long ago."[25]

Hwéeldi, or the place of suffering, was the name the Navajos gave Bosque Redondo. Here, Navajo captives are pictured outside the Issue House at Fort Sumner.

For Navajos, this time in their history was so traumatic and horrific that many refused to speak of it for decades. In fact, elders' narratives first became public when the Navajo tribe was preparing its land claims case before the U.S. Indian Claims Commission in the 1950s, when researchers began recording oral testimony to be used in the hearings. Over nearly a century, since the return from Bosque Redondo, the People had preserved their stories. However, it has never been easy. Of their great misgivings of speaking of these stories, Mary Pioche said, "When men and women talk about Hwéeldi [Bosque Redondo], they say it is something you cannot really talk about, or they say that they would rather not talk about it. Every time their thoughts go back to Hwéeldi, they remember their relatives, families, and friends who were killed by the enemy."[26] Gus Bighorse, who lived in the western part of the Navajo homeland and was a member of Manuelito's band, said of the U.S. Army's war against his people, "We take our tragic story with us, but we can't talk about it. It is so terrible. Only if somebody would ask us a question, then we talk about it."[27] Frank Nez, a Navajo from Tohatchi, New Mexico, said of his ancestors' ordeal during this time, "Nihimásáni dóó nihicheii tih dahooznii. T'áá ałtsxo bikei tiháahooznii. Ch'éi náh yik'ei tihdahooznii."[28] (Our grandmothers and grandfathers suffered greatly. Everything that could be suffered and endured on this earth, they suffered and endured. The stresses were so great.)

The People's stories tell of how their ancestors knew that they could not survive the unbearable living conditions created by Carson's scorch-and-burn policy, and so they made their way to the U.S. forts hoping for some relief. Chahadineli Benally was 85 years old when he told his grandmother's story.[29] During the fearing time, which is what Navajos called the invasion of their land, Benally's relatives lived near Black Mesa, in present-day northeastern Arizona. One day, the young woman who would become his grandmother, was looking for food with her little brother when suddenly a group of Mexicans appeared on horseback. In vain, the young pair tried to hide, but it was too late. The Mexicans had already seen them. With the two Navajos in their custody, the raiders traveled past Ganado and Klagetoh. Thereafter, the land was strange to the frightened pair. As the group made camp that night, the woman did her best to comfort her frightened brother. Eventually, the travelers reached their destination, and the woman became a servant to a Mexican family. She was fortunate in that the woman of the household befriended her, for she was pregnant and she had begun to show. Her new friend was incensed that the young Navajo woman had been stolen from her family, especially because it appeared that she was to be sold to another household. Unknown to her husband, the Mexican woman helped her new friend escape. On her journey home, the young Navajo woman faced many ordeals where she could have easily been killed. Near starvation and extremely weak, she was forced to abandon her newborn infant, which she never forgot. Her brother was never heard from again.

Howard W. Gorman of Ganado, Arizona, also shared stories from his family.[30] As Kit Carson's army moved through Navajo territory, they destroyed sheep and horses. They destroyed the waterholes. The Diné tried to warn others, and families traveled to Tséyi' for safety, walking all night, throughout the next morning, and into the late afternoon. Once they had reached the canyon walls, they stopped and made a fire. They could not continue their journey toward safety, because the steps leading into the canyon were slippery with ice. The exhausted group settled down for the night. By stopping for the night, they enabled the soldiers, who were being guided by a Navajo man, to catch up with them. The Diné fought back but many died that day. One man named Preparing a Warrior escaped by jumping into the canyon. He landed on some bushes and ran to safety. During the melee, a child who had been strapped in a cradle was left behind. However, she was saved from physical harm because of the cradle. One man was wounded and taken captive. He was told very sternly that he must go into the canyon and warn the others that if they did not immediately surrender, Carson's men would kill them. With that message, 16 Navajos came out of the canyon. Many of the Navajos knew that resistance was futile because their traditional enemies the Utes had also joined the New Mexican volunteers and were looking to kill the Navajos. Indeed, to the People, it seems that all of their enemies had been unleashed upon them, and they had only the Holy People to guide them.

PREPARING FOR THE LONG WALK

In the midst of such chaos, the frightened Navajos arrived at the U.S. military posts. At the end of 1863, as it became obvious that the days were getting colder and the nights longer, thousands entered Fort Defiance. In October 1864, more than 7,000 prisoners at Bosque Redondo had exhausted the available supplies. In addition to cutting the already meager rations in half—12 ounces of grain meal and 8 ounces of meat—Carleton ordered that the transportation of prisoners to the reservation be halted. By February 1864, 1,000 prisoners waited transportation to Bosque Redondo. Ten days later, the numbers swelled to 2,500, far outnumbering the garrison of 335 officers and troops. The expanding numbers caught the U.S. Army completely unprepared. Carleton wrote to his superiors about the Navajos' condition: "The weather was very inclement, with terrible gales of wind and heavy falls of snow; the Indians were nearly naked; and, besides many died from dysentery . . ."[31]

U.S. officials tried to assure the Diné that life would be good at their new home. Because they were arriving in the late fall and early winter, they would be given food because they would not have time to plant crops; but when spring came, they could clear the land and plant their crops. They would build homes in the American style—close to each other—and the children would go to school to learn American ways. It all sounded promising, especially as Dinétah was smoldering with Carson's war. Tragically, as the People waited at the fort for the caravan to begin its journey, 126 prisoners died.

It was at the forts that the People were first introduced to new foods, many of which became staples, such as white flour, pork, beans, sugar, and coffee. Prior to the introduction of these foods, Navajos prepared all sorts of corn dishes,

By the end of 1864, more than 7,000 Navajos had been brought to Bosque Redondo, and the U.S. Army realized that it was ill equipped to handle such a large number of prisoners. Here, the U.S. Army Signal Corps guards Navajo captives at Fort Sumner.

including puddings, cakes, breads, steamed corn on the cob, and stews. Because they preferred to keep their wealth on the hoof, they did not often butcher a goat or sheep for meat. When they did, no part of the animal was wasted. To add variety to their diets, they hunted deer and antelope and jerked venison for use during the winter. They flavored their meat dishes with herbs, wild onions, and celery. Berries made excellent puddings while dried squash rinds cut into rings and peaches were stored for later use. In the fall, piñon nuts were collected, roasted, and then stored.

Accustomed to a diet that relied on corn, meat from their stock and wild game, and wild plants for vegetables, they were puzzled with the strange foods given to them as rations. They attempted to eat the white flour by mixing it with water to make a mush. Oftentimes the flour was stale and filled with bugs and even plaster. So they fried the dough in order to make it edible. Ironically, today, "fried bread," a favorite with Navajos and tourists alike, is considered a "traditional" Navajo food. The boiled coffee beans did not grow softer like the beans did. They threw away the dark water and ate the coffee beans. The beef and pork were often rancid and inedible. These new foods made them sick and many died from diarrhea and dysentery.

THE FORCED MARCHES TO BOSQUE REDONDO

The next phase of the Navajos' ordeal would be hell on earth. The "Long Walk" was a series of forced marches that occurred over the course of three years. Historians have recorded no less than 53 separate episodes where Navajos were transported from their homeland to Bosque Redondo, which was created to indoctrinate Navajos to white American ways. These caravans all headed to Albuquerque but then followed several different routes to reach Bosque Redondo. The earlier groups traveled past Santa Fe and Galisteo and went on to Fort Union in northern New Mexico. The Fort Union route, beginning at Fort Defiance, was the longest of the trails at 425 miles. By the shortest route, and the one that was infrequently used, the Navajo prisoners faced a march of 375 miles. The Mountain route—which extended east from Albuquerque through Tijeras Canyon and turned north along the eastern slopes of the Sandias and into Galisteo—became the most frequently used route after Carson's sweep of the Navajo fortress. At Galisteo, the prisoners then proceeded to Fort Union.

The time it took for the trains to reach their Fort Sumner destination varied and depended on the number of prisoners, the weather, and the humanity of the military escorts.

On average, a wagon train might move 10 miles one day and then 15 on another day. In one case, the military commander in charge was so relentless that he drove his captives at least 20 miles each day. He lost many of his prisoners—some managed to escape while others met their death or were stolen by slave raiders. A few wagons carried the elderly, pregnant women, and children, but mostly they were used to carry military supplies. The captives walked with the soldiers prodding them forward with their rifles and guns.

The first group of captives left for Bosque Redondo when Carson's summer campaign of 1863 was in its opening phase. On or about August 6, Captain Albert H. Pfeiffer captured eight Navajos, including five women and children. The captives were taken to Fort Defiance and then to Fort Wingate. At Fort Wingate, 43 Navajos from the Dine' Ana'ii Sandoval's band joined the captives. Although the Dine' Ana'ii had allied with the New Mexicans and then the Americans, they were among the first to be relocated to the reservation on the Pecos River. The commander in charge of moving the group to Bosque Redondo had his orders: If any of the captives attempted to escape, they were to be shot. None did. On September 2, the captives passed through Santa Fe. Santa Fe's newspaper, the *Weekly Gazette*, printed its observation of the captives' passing: "We presume they will be transferred to some military post to the East of this, and there retained separated from . . . the balance of the tribe to the end of the war."[32] On September 7, the prisoners arrived at Fort Union. Here, the officer in charge reported the death of a child; hundreds more would follow, adding to the unknown number who would perish during the forced removal. The death of a woman was also reported. Five days later, the prisoners arrived at Fort Union and moved out on September 10. In the 24 days since their departure from Fort Wingate, they arrived at their destination.

Two months after this first group arrived at Bosque Redondo, another train of 200 captives arrived, which included the headman Delgadito and his band. Leaders like Delgadito sought to alleviate their people's suffering, and at the same time, acted as a source of hope and inspiration when they decided to surrender at the forts. Under the command of Captain Rafael Chacon, Delgadito and his band left Fort Wingate; however, upon reaching the outskirts of Santa Fe, Lieutenant V. B. Wardwell assumed responsibility. Wardwell's report is one of the few that provides a detailed account of the train's daily movements. As the captives arrived on the outskirts of Santa Fe on the afternoon of November 22, the temperature dropped below freezing as a storm shrouded the route ahead. Each day the captives traveled 8 to 10 miles. The first night outside of Santa Fe they made camp in the hills east of town. Over the coming days, the group stopped each night at Kozlowski's Ranch, San José, Tecolote, Las Vegas, and William Kroenig's Ranch on Sapello Creek and then about two and half miles southwest of Watrous. At Fort Union, Captain William P. Calloway assumed the responsibility for the captives and forced them onto the last leg of the journey.

On December 10, Delgadito and his band arrived at Bosque Redondo. Fifteen members of his band were missing and had probably been stolen by slave raiders. At the fort, Navajos who were already at the prison camp greeted the newly arrived captives with much emotion. At this time, the fort consisted of tents and small adobe huts. The post commander, Major Wallen, reported to his superiors that his Navajo wards were comfortably quartered in old Sibley tents. A third train of captives also passed through Fort Union on the way to Fort Sumner. As historian Frank McNitt has observed, this route was especially arduous and no explanation has been found for using this longer route.[33]

A few months later, Delgadito and three other men returned to their homeland with Carleton's message that all Diné must surrender or be given no mercy. The headman urged his fellow Navajos to surrender. He informed them that he had been to Bosque Redondo, and compared to the count-less number of Navajos dying around him, the newly created reservation was a sanctuary. At the end of January, Delga-dito arrived at Fort Wingate with 680 Navajos, and a few days later, around 500 more joined them. Once they realized that the U.S. Army would not kill them and that they might live, they came into the forts. Degaldito reported that along the trail to the fort, a party of Mexicans attacked them and cap-tured women, children, and livestock. Several of the warriors had also been killed at they tried to defend the band.

By early 1864, the number of Navajos surrendering at the forts in Navajo country reached such proportions that the U.S. Army found itself ill prepared. On February 27, Carleton reported to General Thomas in Washington, "What with the Navajoes I have captured and those who have surrendered we have now more than 3,000, and will, without doubt, soon have the whole tribe." He continued, "You have doubtless seen the last of the Navajo war, a war that has been continued with but few intermissions for 180 years." He declared, "this formidable band of robbers and murderers have at last been made to succumb."[34] Because of the large numbers, Carleton ordered the caravans to travel the mountain route. The cap-tives found a bit of relief because arroyos—narrow valleys and the canyons between the mountains and mesas—provided some shelter from the winter elements. Adequate supplies of water and wood were found. Also, for the army's purposes, this route made it possible to access emergency supplies, and surveillance was easier for the garrisons. Several other large contingents of prisoners also marched along this particular route. In February 1864, a train of nearly 1,500 men, women, and children traveled this route. Following on the heels of this train, a column of 2,500 prisoners also followed this route.

New Mexican citizens were aware of the Navajo prisoners passing near the towns of Albuquerque and Santa Fe. While few notices were written down or printed in newspapers such as the *Santa Fe Gazette*, the town's citizens watched one column of prisoners trail past the village but they were not moved to sympathy or compassion. Blaming the Navajos for the cycles of violence that characterized the southwest, many of the citizens added to the prisoners' misery by stealing women and children who had let their vigilance slip for a moment. In the nineteenth century, New Mexican settlers, including incoming white Americans, believed that native people were savages who deserved to be exterminated, and if not that, then removed far away from white civilization.

Peshlakai Etsedi's Story

In 1963, Peshlakai Etsedi, which translates as "Silversmith," told his story to Sallie Pierce Brewer of the Museum of Northern Arizona.[35] Peshlakai, who was from the Arizona region of Navajo country, was a boy when his kin were rounded up to go to Bosque Redondo. At first, his family attempted to elude enemies like the Utes, but with the reports that their country was being decimated, they prepared to go to the forts, for it was unsafe in their homeland. Before they began the journey to Fort Wingate, the medicine man conducted a ceremony for their protection and prayed for all of the people. After another day had passed, they started toward the fort and passed a Zuni village, where some Zunis, who were their old enemies, greeted them. The Zunis declared that could offer the weary travelers respite from their journey if they would accompany them back to their village. As the tired and hungry Navajos thought about the invitation, a lone Zuni man appeared and warned them to leave immediately, for the other men intended to kill the adults and take the children captive. A strange white man appeared and affirmed the Zunis' warning. For Peshlakai's group, this was the first time they had ever seen a white man. Alerted, they hastened their travel eastward toward the fort, but the Zuni warriors began moving against them. Just as it looked like their enemies might catch them, men in blue coats appeared on horses. The men, who turned out to be U.S. soldiers, circled the Zuni men and pushed them away from the fleeing Navajos.

The Navajos joined a caravan going to Fort Sumner. As they traveled toward Albuquerque, the women and children were placed in wagons while Pesklaki decided to walk because the wagons moved slowly. Along the way, his mother's uncle, an elder, died and the soldiers buried him. Once the train reached the outskirts of Albuquerque, they were herded into a large corral, where other Navajo prisoners waited. There, they were given corn, bread, and meat. The captives reached Bosque Redondo in about 34 days. At Bosque Redondo, they were once again herded into a large corral and given rations. At the camp, relatives who had made the march two years earlier greeted them and took them to live with them.

Other Navajo Narratives of the Forced March

Many other narratives that Navajos told in the 1960s and 1970s relate their ancestors' experiences on the trail of the Long Walk. Keyah David said that in his family there is the story of how a couple were having trouble keeping up with the rest of the group because their infant was growing weaker and weaker. Soon the wife fell farther and farther behind with her baby while her husband urged her to walk faster. The others would soon be out of sight and they would be left to the dangers that lurked around them. Out of desperation, he entreated his wife to abandon the seemingly unconscious child, for it seemed that he would not live much longer. When she refused, he said angrily, "All right, stay there if you like, but I'm going on. The baby is going to die anyway."[36] As the man hurried to catch up to the group, he thought of an idea. Breaking off the stalks of cactus oozing juice, he took it back to his wife and their baby and fed the liquid to the infant. The infant stirred, the father broke off more cactus stalks, and with his family, hurried to catch up with the slow moving caravan.

A report dated December 1863 notes that as the caravan of prisoners left San Jose at sunrise and then set up camp at Tecolote, one of the Navajos known as an idiot refused to leave. A U.S. soldier enjoined three other Navajo men to return for him, whereupon they refused, saying, "It is better for us to be rid of him, and we all hope he may be frozen to death or killed, as he is a fool and always has troubled us."[37] Prisoners seem to have lost all humanity, which Navajo accounts also reflect; however, the captives' responses to what was happening to them and how they sometimes treated each other gives an indication of the truly horrific circumstances in which they found themselves, for indeed they had been reduced to beings less than animals by the U.S. military.

Other Navajos told of how women and children rode in wagons while the blue-coated soldiers rode alongside them. John Daw testified before the U.S. Land Claims Commission in 1951 and reported that his parents had told him that when people became exhausted along the forced march, the soldiers would become harsh, rebuff them, and if one persisted, he was shot to death. Daw also noted the violence shown to the women: "These soldiers did not have any regard for the women folks. They took unto themselves for wives somebody else's wife, and many times the Navajo man whose wife was being taken tried to ward off the soldiers, but immediately he was shot and killed and they took his wife."[38] John Bowman, another Navajo who testified before the commission reported that, "The children would get exhausted from the day's walk and want to ride on these wagons . . . and if the children were a little bit too large or a little older and able to walk, the soldiers would just cast them aside and make them walk until the time came when they would dispose of them."[39] Other storytellers note that the U.S. military was not consistent in their treatment of the prisoners. For example, sometimes they would allow a Navajo family member to bury his or her dead; and in other cases, refuse to allow the captives to

While some Navajo women and children were permitted to ride in wagons during the Long Walk, many were forced to walk and were often abused by the U.S. soldiers who accompanied them on the journey. Here, a Navajo woman carries a baby on her back while at Bosque Redondo.

stop and prod them to move on. Sometimes bodies were left to be eaten by wild animals. All of these stories are filled with such pain, humiliation, and degradation, that those who hear and learn of them cannot help but reflect upon the lengths the Navajos went in order to survive.

Francis McCabe's Group of Prisoners

Captain Francis McCabe left with approximately 800 prisoners from Fort Defiance on March 20, 1864. He only had 23 wagons at his disposal, hardly enough to adequately transport the prisoners. Rations amounting to one pound of meat or flour, and a half-pound of bacon meant to last for eight days were soon consumed. The next day, the Navajos in McCabe's group were forced to continue their march in a severe snowstorm that lasted four days. McCabe refused to stop, to the great distress of the prisoners. Reaching Fort Wingate did not solve their problems; for the army could only offer McCabe's party a half-pound each of flour and beef for each captive. He also failed to receive additional clothing and wagons, both of which had been promised. Fearful of a revolt, McCabe called in the headmen and assured them that full rations would be received at the next stop, Los Pinos, near Albuquerque. As the party traveled past the villages of Acoma and Laguna, McCabe noted that a few of the Pueblo people came out and attempted to provide some assistance to the captives. McCabe ordered his men to watch the columns to make sure that the Navajos did not leave with their Pueblo allies. Finally, the caravan reached Los Pinos, where they were able to rest before they began the next leg of the journey. Upon their arrival at Fort Sumner, McCabe recounted the Navajos' relief: "On getting sight of the reservation, with its ploughed and planted fields, its numerous acequias through which the water flowed and sparkled, and the green meadows on either side of the Pecos River, where horses, cattle, and sheep were quietly grazing, the Navajoes were greatly delighted and expressed great satisfaction with what they saw . . . I noticed a spirit of activity and industry amongst them, which promises well for their rapid and complete civilization." [40] Leaving on April 24, the captives reached Bosque Redondo on May 11. McCabe estimated that 110 Navajos had died while 25 had escaped.

MANUELITO AND BARBONCITO ARRIVE AT BOSQUE REDONDO

By May 31, 1864, Captain H. B. Bristol reported that a total of 5,174 Navajos were at the reservation. Of these, about a third were children and infants. By August of that year, the number of captives swelled to 7,137. As previously mentioned, Manuelito, who had become a symbol of Navajo resistance to the U.S. Army and New Mexicans, had turned himself in earlier but then had escaped and remained in his homeland until 1866. In June 1866, three women from his band arrived at Fort Sumner with their children and relatives. They reported that Manuelito had been badly wounded in the left forearm and left side in a fight with Hopis.[41] Finally, Manuelito, wounded and weak, surrendered at Fort Wingate. On September 9, he and his remaining band, which had dwindled from 500 to 23, began the arduous journey to Bosque Redondo. Constant harassments by slave raiders had resulted in the loss of many of his band, including his own children and his brothers and sisters. His wife Juanita remained at his side throughout the years that he remained in hiding. Determined to make an example of this great Diné leader, Carleton sent him through the outskirts of Santa Fe, intending to parade him in front of New Mexican citizens. The *Santa Fe Gazette* noted Manuelito's passing: "Manuelito and his band and quite a large part of his band were brought to Santa Fe last week. They are to be taken to Bosque Redondo and furnished a new home where they will have less of the cares of the State on their minds and more bread and meat to eat. Manuelito was the most stubborn of all the Navajo Chiefs and was the most difficult to be brought to terms."[42] Not long after Manuelito's surrender, the peace leader Barboncito took his people to Bosque Redondo. The last large caravan of 417 prisoners was taken to the Pecos on December 13, 1866, when they left Fort Wingate. As this group approached the Rio Grande near Albuquerque,

Carleton sent instructions to the commanding officer at the Albuquerque post: "I am afraid that the parties of Navajos who come in, and are sent by you from Albuquerque via Cañon Blanco to the Bosque Redondo, will, at this season of the year, suffer for want of fuel and of shelter of bluffs and groves by that routing . . ."[43] Carleton then directed future captives to be directed through another route that went through Tijeras, near Galisteo and then onto the mountain route. This group of captives brought with them approximately 300 horses and the same amount of sheep and goats.

DESERTIONS AND CRITICISM

Because Carleton's vision of Bosque Redondo was far from realistic—prisoners continued to suffer from heat, hunger, disease, and cold, among other maladies—groups of Navajos began deserting. First, on May 1, 1864, it was reported that about 43 captives had fled. Next, on April 30, 1865, about 900 Navajos left. And then on June 14, more than 1,000 Navajos also escaped, and on July 15, another unknown number escaped. On November 23, 1865, the Mescalero Apaches fled and returned to their homeland. They had not gotten along with their Navajo cousins at the reservation. On July 31, October 2, and September 27, 1867, U.S. military officers reported more desertions. It is difficult, if not impossible, to ascertain exactly how many Navajos returned to the Pecos, because they had discovered that Dinétah was still filled with raiders looking for Navajo women and children.

Soon after his successful campaign against the Navajos, Kit Carson requested leave of his duties, for it had been a long time since he had seen his wife and children. In late April 1864, the Indian fighter relinquished his command of the Navajo expedition and returned to Taos. For a brief period, he oversaw Fort Sumner but resigned after three months. While Carson helped the U.S. Army defeat the Navajos, it was not through a series of battles; rather, his use of guerrilla

Although he was often celebrated as a national hero for leading John C. Fremont's famous expeditions to the West in the 1840s, Christopher Kit Carson is reviled by Navajos for destroying their homeland and forcing them to relocate to Bosque Redondo. Today, Navajo leaders such as New Mexico state senator Leonard Tsosie are successfully challenging Carson's legacy as a heroic frontiersman.

warfare proved fatal to the Navajo resistance. Today, Carson remains a controversial figure, especially in New Mexico, where Navajos and other Native Americans have steadfastly challenged any attempts to memorialize him. For the Diné, Kit Carson, along with James Carleton, remain the symbol of American aggression and inhumanity against all native people who stood in the way of manifest destiny.

Bosque Redondo (Hwéeldi)

ON JUNE 4, 2005, NAVAJOS AND THEIR SUPPORTERS gathered at Fort Sumner to celebrate the official opening of the Bosque Redondo Memorial, which includes a museum and visitor center. Before the museum was built, a small building served as park ranger headquarters and featured a modest display of photographs, including ones of Fort Sumner in the 1860s. Very little evidence remains of the original fort that was established by Brigadier General James Carleton in 1863. Along the Pecos River, a few trees and brush line its banks. Floods in 1904, 1937, and 1941 have washed away almost all traces of military and Navajo presence. In 1863, however, the area around Fort Sumner was much different. The banks of the Pecos River bustled with activity as U.S. troops cut down trees for buildings and firewood and inspected the area to determine its suitability for irrigating and planting crops. Would this be a good place to relocate the Mescaleros and Navajos?

A PLAN OF ASSIMILATION

Carleton established the site as a reservation where the assimilation of the Mescaleros and the Navajos to American ways would begin. In the nineteenth century, native people's resistance to white American expansion made federal officials and military officers remark that it was less costly to remove native peoples from their traditional homelands than to exterminate them outright. Once relocated, native peoples could begin the process of indoctrination. Carleton was known to his constituents as the "Christian general" and a humanitarian who believed that Christian and moral instruction of native peoples would ensure that they would be accepted into American society. As a man of his time, he followed federal Indian policies for dealing with native peoples, meaning that they should become "white men." However, from the Navajo perspective, to call Carleton and other white men of his time "Christians" and "humanitarians" is to overlook the violence and atrocities that Navajos met when they challenged American expansionist policies.

On October 31, 1862, Carleton established a military post on the Pecos River at a point known as Bosque Redondo, which means "round grove." The site was 110 miles southeast of present-day Las Vegas, New Mexico, and 160 miles east of Albuquerque. The general named the post in honor of his former commander Edwin V. Sumner. Previously, herders had grazed their livestock at the site and a trading post had conducted business in the 1850s. Carleton thought the new post would offer protection to New Mexicans who wanted to graze their animals and serve as a barrier to protect settlers from Kiowas and Comanches coming from the Texas plains, as well as Mescaleros coming from the south. Contrary to Carleton's desires, a board reported that a site approximately 45 miles upstream was a better choice. The recommended site had an abundance of wood, clear drinking water, and was not on a flood plain, all of which Carleton ignored.

In December 1862, the fledging fort consisted of tents and housed six officers and 133 enlisted men. The site's poor living conditions, combined with other factors, such as its distance from a supply center such as Fort Union, the constant shortage of food for Navajo and Apache captives, the continued hostilities among Navajos, Apaches, and New Mexicans, and the dreary weather, made the reservation doomed to fail. Perhaps even more significant to the reservation's failure, the Mescaleros and the Navajos always looked to the day when they could return to their homeland.

The Mescalero Apaches, suffering from the cold and starving, arrived at Bosque Redondo in early December 1862. The first task they were given was to build shelters for themselves. At the same time, the soldiers were busy constructing stables, warehouses, a hospital, and other necessary buildings. In early January 1863, more Mescaleros arrived from Fort Stanton. In addition to making their own shelters, they were also expected to begin farming. By June, they had cleared, plowed, and planted more than 200 acres of corn, beans, and melons. On the one hand, the U.S. Army expected the Mescaleros to embrace American values of industriousness through farming and virtue through Christianity and western education, but on the other hand, they also realized that funding the Apaches' upkeep would be difficult. Indeed, the captives were expected to labor in the fields as a way to cut the costs of maintaining the reservation. The men began the laborious work of digging irrigation ditches; because there were few proper tools available, they used their hands to work the soil. When Superintendent Michael Steck visited the reservation, he explained to Indian agent Lorenzo Labadie that his department could not furnish full rations and that the Mescaleros should be allowed to hunt to supplement their rations. On one successful hunt, the Mescalero men bagged 86 antelopes. However, with the arrival of the Navajo prisoners in late 1863, the Apaches found that they had to compete with the more numerous Navajos for the scarce resources.

Another issue that compounded the difficulties of smooth operations at the reservation, and which were part of the reason for its failure to thrive, was the feuding between the war and Indian departments about who should be responsible for the prisoners. When the first contingent of Navajos arrived at the fort, New Mexico superintendent Michael Steck, who was a steadfast critic of Carleton, ordered Labadie to refuse to take charge of the new arrivals. Steck took every opportunity to criticize Carleton. He pointed out the high cost of operating Bosque Redondo and its unsuitable location and argued that the Navajo population and the numbers of their livestock overburdened the land. Besides, added Steck, despite the fact that they were related, the Apaches and the Navajos were traditional enemies and there would always be hostilities between the two groups. He continually urged that the Navajos be settled in their own country.

CONDITIONS AT BOSQUE REDONDO

In anticipation of the Navajos' arrival in late 1863, Carleton advertised for meat and foodstuffs in New Mexican newspapers. Some of the items he requested included shelled corn, with a delivery of 1,000 fanegas as early as December. (A fanega equaled 140 pounds). He also ordered additional shipments of shelled corn to be sent in January and March 1864. In the coming months, additional supplies would be ordered, including wheat meal, corn meal, and heads of cattle and other livestock. Carleton was so determined that his program would succeed that at times he ordered all military commanders to reduce soldiers' rations—to ensure availability for the captives.

Over the course of the next few years, Carleton would come under fire for awarding supply contracts to his supporters. Many of these contractors profited enormously from selling supplies and food for Bosque Redondo. Some of Carleton's supporters argued that the cost of buying supplies, including beef, could only be good, because New Mexico's economy would flourish. In June, Labadie reported that the flour provided to the Mescaleros was unfit for consumption. The contractor William H. Moore, a prominent New Mexican and a mining speculator, had sold flour with bits of slate, broken dried bread, and a mixture that looked like plaster of Paris in it. Other supplies coming into the reservation would be reported to be of "livid quality."[44]

The first photographs of Navajos were taken at Bosque Redondo and became available to Navajos themselves in the 1960s and 1970s, when white researchers published some of the photographs and primary documents in the *Navajo Times*, a tribally owned newspaper. In 1980, white educator Robert Roessel Jr. published a collection of photographs from the Fort Sumner period.[45] In addition to military reports and Navajo narratives, these photographs give some indication of how Navajo captives fared at the reservation.

Some of the pressing problems that the captives faced as soon as they arrived included the lack of adequate shelter, the constant shortage of food, the harsh climate, and bouts of epidemic diseases, all of which took their toll. In the hopes of changing their living patterns, federal officials expected the captives to live in homes situated close together, much in the manner that the Pueblo peoples lived. The Diné, pastoralists and farmers who lived in extended family networks, were accustomed to living miles apart from their neighbors. So, of course, they refused to live in such tight-knit quarters. However, there was little attention paid to providing them with adequate housing. In the photographs, Navajo dwellings are simply pits that had been dug into the ground and

During their time at Bosque Redondo, many Navajo men were forced to construct buildings at Fort Sumner for the U.S. Army. Here, U.S. troops oversee Navajo workers as they build barracks for the troops.

then covered with brush. Navajo storyteller Dugal Tsosie Begay said of the living conditions, "Most homes at Fort Sumner . . . were made by digging holes in the ground. Laid across the holes were logs and branches. On top of the logs and branches were piles of dirt."[46] In contrast, the soldiers and officers lived more comfortably in barracks that had been built with adobe. Photographs show Navajos working on the buildings meant for the soldiers' use and others show wood stacked against the walls. Because reports from the soldiers and Navajos indicate that the captives often had to walk miles, sometimes as far away as 25 miles, in order to find enough wood to warm themselves and had to resort to burning greasewood bushes, the wood stacked alongside the adobe buildings was mostly likely reserved for the exclusive use of the military personnel.

The Navajos' refusal to live in shelters constructed next to each other was compounded by their beliefs about death and dead bodies. They refused to enter any establishment where a person had died. Frustrated with the captives' avowal to follow their own rules, Carleton finally agreed that families could abandon their shelter if a family member died and then build a new shelter at the end of the row. The hospital, upon completion, had nine small rooms, including a kitchen and two rooms reserved for surgery. The hospital had few patients, for the Navajos continually refused to enter any establishment where a person had died. In the spring of 1864, there were outbreaks of catarrh and dysentery. Over the course of their four years at Bosque Redondo, the Navajos and Apaches would be afflicted with various diseases, including pneumonia, typhoid, dysentery, pleurisy, skin problems such as erysipelas, and rheumatism. Also, deadly epidemics of smallpox, measles, and cholera struck the post. For the Diné, death became a daily occurrence; moreover, their population did not increase. In May 1864, the census revealed that only three births had been reported. In that same month, the census showed that a total of 5,182 Navajos were living at the reservation.

During their time at Bosque Redondo, the People continued to rely on their own medicine people and even performed, albeit in a limited way due to their location, ceremonies such as the N'da, the Enemy Way. In talking about the performance of the N'da, Dugal Tsosie Begay noted that horses, which were used in the ceremony, were often not available and so people "used sticks as their horses."[47] Other ceremonies such as the Mountain Way chant and the Fire Dance also continued to be performed to heal sicknesses. At the same time, many of the Dine noted that medicine people did not have the kinds of ceremonies and medicines that could heal the sicknesses and diseases that the whites had brought.

PROMOTING SELF-SUFFICIENCY

Part of Carleton's plan included making the Navajos more self-sufficient, especially because Congress's appropriations were limited and supplies were unreliable. Further, native men often attacked the incoming freight trains and took the supplies for their own use. Ironically, Carleton, like the Americans and New Mexicans of his time, refused to recognize that the Navajos, who had held the balance of power in the southwest for more than a century, had been a wealthy and autonomous people in charge of their own destiny. Now their fate was in the hands of their conquerors, who wanted the Navajos to rely on the reservation agent. Because the captives began arriving in the late fall of 1863 and into the early winter of 1864, there had been no time to work the land and make it ready for spring planting. Relying on rations, Carleton ordered the fort commander to have the Navajo men prepare the land for planting. In addition, the work of digging an irrigation ditch would keep them occupied. He stated that in order to have a plentiful harvest, eight plows had to constantly till the soil, from March 1 to June 10 for corn, and to July 10 for beans and other crops. The Navajo agent reported with satisfaction that his charges had done an impressive job, digging miles of ditches. Carleton was so enthusiastic about his program that he reported in the spring of 1864 that indeed Navajos and Mescaleros were moving toward self-sufficiency; that all was going as he had planned at Bosque Redondo. In later years, American historians would declare that Navajos had constructed one of the most intricate and best-engineered irrigation systems in all of New Mexico. These historians would also declare that while the Navajos were at the reservation, they had acquired new technologies, replacing the digging stick with hoes, shovels,

Despite limited access to wool at Bosque Redondo, Navajo women continued to weave wearing blankets and articles of clothing by using bayeta cloth, which they would unravel and re-spin. Throughout their people's history, Navajo women have used textiles as a means to preserve their culture.

rakes, and plows and had learned about metal work to make nails, horse and mule shoes, and, of course, jewelry.

In another attempt to promote Navajo self-sufficiency, the Indian agent encouraged the women to continue weaving at their looms, where they created wearing blankets and articles of clothing. Although they had few sheep from which to shear wool, they did manage to weave. In addition to using commercially prepared yarns and dyes, weavers

(continues on page 80)

DAH'IISTŁ'Ó: NAVAJO TEXTILES

For as far back as they can remember, Navajos have always woven textiles. These textiles embody values linked to the land, the natural world, livestock, family, and extended kin. As many a weaver will attest, weaving is a process that manifests the rich, expansive, and complex belief system of the Diné and expresses the central concept of K'e—proper and respectful relationships to the world and to each other. Taking care of livestock is a full-time endeavor that involves all family members, including children who learn the virtues of hard work and responsibility through sheep herding. To ensure the prosperity of the land and family, livestock is also blessed during Blessingway ceremonies. Navajo weavers explain that their grandmothers were given the knowledge and skill to weave from Grandmother Spider during the creation of the world. Elder weavers then passed on their knowledge of how to fashion the looms, to shear, spin, and dye the wool. They shared the songs and prayers associated with weaving with their daughters who conveyed them to their daughters.

By the eighteenth century, the textiles woven by Navajo women had become popular trade items throughout the southwest. As early as 1705, Spaniards noted the quality of the textiles, which were highly prized as wearing blankets that soon came to be known as "chief's blankets." Although it is difficult to document, women, as weavers of these durable and waterproof textiles, were directly involved in the trade relations that existed between tribal peoples and then the Spaniards. The few samples of Navajo weaving from the eighteenth century are simple in design and show evidence of trade with the Spaniards, including the use of indigo blue dyes in the wearing blankets.

The textiles also reflect the transformation that Navajos experienced in the mid-nineteenth century. First, the slave trade centered on the taking of Navajo women and children who entered New Mexican households as servants and peons. In these households, they continued to weave and produced textiles now called "slave blankets." When the Diné were taken to Hwéeldi, they had few sheep so wool was scarce. Undaunted, they took red bayeta cloth, which was part of the annuities distribution, unraveled and respun the wool, and then incorporated it into their weavings. Textiles woven during the time they were at Bosque Redondo evoke many memories for weavers today. For example, textiles display patterns show the anguish the captives experienced during their exile. Other textiles tell stories of Monster Slayer's and Born for Water's journey in search of their father.

In the 1880s, a railroad connecting the east and west coasts was built through Dinétah, bringing to Navajos the beginnings of a tourism-based economy. Prior to 1868, textiles had been utilitarian and an important source of wealth for Navajos. By the end of the nineteenth century, the textiles became smaller in size for the tourist market. Traders, working with entrepreneurs, travelers, photographers, and writers, created a national market for Navajo textiles. Non-Indians bought the smaller pieces as throw rugs and souvenirs that would remind them of their travels to the "exotic" southwest. Although a select number of weavers like Elle of Ganado were able to make a living from their weaving, most weavers were poorly paid.

Today, women continue to weave, and in some communities, such as Crownpoint and Ramah, New Mexico, they have established weaving co-ops in order to preserve the tradition. They find that teaching their art to the next generation is one way to create continuity with the Navajo past. Moreover, male weavers have garnered public attention, with shows devoted to their accomplishments at major museums throughout North America.

(continued from page 77)

also supplemented available wool with red bayeta cloth, which they unraveled and respun. At Bosque Redondo, the women expanded their designs by incorporating vertically placed, outlined serrated diamonds and uses for their textiles by creating smaller ones that were used as saddle blankets. While Navajo woven textiles are often believed to be created for an outside market and prior to its commercialization, as utilitarian, scholars Paul Zolbrod and Roseann Willinks further illuminate the sacred meanings of the textiles women wove at Bosque Redondo in their book *Weaving A World: Textiles and the Navajo Way of Seeing*.[48] For example, not only do the textiles embody "mythic" time, but also recorded historical time. One textile, with its pattern of crossing steps and serrated points along its edges, symbolizes the Hero Twins' ordeals to overcome obstacles, in much the same manner that the Navajos overcame military defeat and then removal to the reservation. Other textiles were used in the performance of ceremonies to heal the People.

SHORTAGE OF FOOD

The inadequacies of the "civilizing program" were further evidenced in the amount and kinds of rations supplied to the captives, which consisted of beef, mutton, bacon, beans, white flour, shelled corn, and coffee. In April 1864, the Navajo prisoners were receiving two and a half pounds of meat and flour every fifth day. However, the starving men, women, and children ate their portions, intended to last a week, in two days, leaving them to suffer miserably until the next issuance of rations. Agent Labadie reported of his wards' misery, "They eat their rations in two days, and during the other three days they suffer, eating hides, and begging wherever they can."[49] In his recollections, Howard W. Gorman said of the Navajo people's constant hunger, "The prisoners begged the Army for some corn, and the leaders also pleaded for it for their people." In desperation, boys wandered off to where the mules and horses were corralled and poked around in the manure to take undigested corn out of it. The kernels were roasted in hot ashes and eaten. At times, the captives' rations were often cut in half. Author Gerald Thompson has calculated the caloric intake of the daily issuance of food at 1,000 calories, well below the number needed to sustain a healthy lifestyle. In efforts to control access to food supplies to the starving captives, U.S. Army personnel devised methods that would ensure that each person received their meager share. For example, because the soldiers feared that some Navajos were drawing more than one ration, they created metal ration discs that were to be exchanged for food. However, in desperation, the captives soon learned to create replicas of the discs.

Casting about for ways to supplement the food supply, the Navajo agent authorized the Navajo men to hunt wild game. At another time, when supplies were late, Carleton considered ways to stretch the food, including the construction of ovens to bake loaves of bread. Among the captives were headmen and their families who brought sizeable herds of cattle, sheep, and goats. In several cases, the U.S. Army purchased their livestock, which they distributed to the entire group. Several times Navajo men attacked freight trains and sometimes made off with their cargo. In one attack, the Navajo men ambushed an incoming freight and made off with 5,200 sheep and 13 horses and burros. In this case, the U.S. Army, aided by the Mescaleros, followed them and recovered most of the sheep and provisions. On January 4, 1864, a military officer reported another Navajo attack. The warriors took 60 horses from the Mescalero herd and several cavalry mounts. Determined that the Navajo men would not get away with their prizes, the U.S. Army, again aided by Apaches, went after them in a heavy snowstorm. The pursuers eventually overtook the Navajos about 12 miles south of the fort.

During the running battle, waged over 10 miles, the cavalry and their Apache allies killed about 40 Navajos. While it has often appeared that Navajos were the instigators of attacks on New Mexican settlements and on freight trains going to Bosque Redondo, reports indicate that Navajos were oftentimes the victims of attacks as well. Indeed, one report of an attack on Navajo captives at the reservation in 1867 indicates that they were not safe anywhere.

Because of the severe conditions under which the Diné struggled, some of the women were forced into prostitution to get food. Girls as young as 12 and 13 years old were selling their bodies for a pint of cornmeal from the soldiers. The rise in venereal diseases, particularly syphilis, quickly surpassed malnutrition as the most pressing health problem on the reservation. Blaming the Navajo women, federal officials declared that the women's "loose morals" were the cause of the disease running rampant throughout the fort. In an effort to combat the problem, Carleton ordered that women who lived with soldiers, reported to be "laundresses" and "housekeepers," would no longer receive rations. In contrast, agent Labadie reported that reports of Mescalero women selling their bodies were almost nonexistent. Federal officials surmised that the Mescalero women did not engage in prostitution because of severe penalties by their people, including having the tips of their noses cut off. Indeed, captives went to extreme lengths in order to survive and get food for their families. Moreover, as feminist scholars like Andrea Smith have pointed out, the conquest of America has included the sexual violation of native women and conditions at Bosque Redondo were likely no different.[50]

ESCAPE FROM BOSQUE REDONDO

Despite all of the problems that plagued the reservation, Carleton plodded on with his assimilation plan. On July 17, 1864, Carleton, who was in Santa Fe, wrote to Navajo agent

H. B. Bristol that he had invited three Catholic priests and several nuns to provide Christian instruction to the Mescaleros and Navajos. Writing to Bishop Jean Baptiste Lamy of Santa Fe, Carleton explained that the captives might find Catholicism more to their liking, given the seeming similarity in pageantry. Along with instruction in Christianity, Carleton also believed in educating Navajo children. Like whites of his generation, he thought it impossible to retrain adults; rather, he believed that the younger generation should be the ones to learn about white values. Although there was a school on the reservation, it was not able to provide adequate education. First, the building was poorly constructed and few supplies were available. Second, reluctant parents sent their children only because food was used as an enticement. In March 1865, Carleton again wrote to his superiors requesting help in educating the 3,000 children.

Although Carleton reported to his superiors that Bosque Redondo was a success, in reality, conditions at the reservation were horrendous. Even as territorial governor Henry Connelly praised Carleton, saying that the reservation was a success and the territory was experiencing unprecedented peace, the final six months of 1865 saw serious setbacks, including destroyed harvests, inadequate supplies and rations, low birthrates, and reports that Navajos were continuing to attack New Mexican settlements. On Christmas Eve, 7,800 Navajos were counted to receive distributions of blankets, bolts of cloth, awls, buttons and beads, sheep shears, scissors, knives, hoes, shovels, and axes. The prices for these poor quality items soared, by as much as 100 percent. Carleton refused to address the continual complaints of the state of the supplies received because many of the contractors were his friends and political supporters. Author Gerald Thompson noted the poor conditions on the reservation during the first year: "It was clear that many Navajos would be buried that winter, in the cold strange Pecos country, for want of food and clothing."[51]

On May 1, 1864, the first report of desertions surfaced. Forty-three Navajos disappeared from the reservation, and on April 30, another 900 captives left. In the darkness of night, on June 14, Navajo leaders Ganado Blanco and Barboncito and about 500 members of their bands fled the reservation. Frustrated by the number of Navajos leaving the reservation, Carleton put out an order: Navajos caught outside of the boundaries without a pass were to be punished. When one Navajo man was apprehended 25 miles southeast of Las Vegas and returned to the fort, he was forced to wear a heavy ball and chain for the next two months and endure hard labor.

One April night in 1865, the Apache leader Ojo Blanco fled the reservation with 42 of his band. By May, as these continued desertions began to interfere with the operation of the reservation, the rest of the Mescaleros left in the darkness of night to return to their homeland. They executed a brilliant plan where they broke into several small groups and scattered in several directions. Unable to decide which group to chase, the U.S. Army admitted failure and returned to the post without the Mescaleros. In May 1865, it was reported that more than 1,000 Navajos had left the reservation. At the same time, captives were still arriving from Navajo country. By 1867, more and more captives were reported missing from the reservation. Sometimes the soldiers were sent to look for the fleeing Navajos, while others escaped with little notice. Returning to their homeland was an ordeal fraught with danger, for not only were the Navajos unfamiliar with the landscape, but they faced danger from animals, as well as slave raiders.

It is not known exactly how many Navajos journeyed to Bosque Redondo, or the numbers that escaped to return to their homeland. Many probably returned to the reservation after seeing the poor living conditions in the homeland. Also up for conjecture is the number of Navajos who did not go to Bosque Redondo; the numbers have been estimated as high as half of the Navajo population, thereby putting the Navajo population in the mid-nineteenth century at approximately 16,000. Gus Bighorse, who was from the northwestern region of Dinétah and who rode with Manuelito's band, said that many of his clan members did not go to Hwéeldi. Others who lived mainly in the western and northwestern regions of Navajo country, now northern Arizona and southeastern Utah, hid in the canyons and atop almost inaccessible mountains. Navajo elder Ernest Nelson told his story, saying, "My own ancestors did not go on the Long Walk," and "When enemies came for them they flew down into the canyon gorge behind Navajo Mountain."[52] Historian Peter Iverson has assessed the significance of those Navajos who remained in Navajo country, writing that their continual presence strengthened Navajo claims to the land, which would be recognized in the years after 1868, when the land base was expanded several times through presidential executive orders.[53] These Navajos were also important in revitalizing the economy, because they had planted their fields and cared for their livestock when their kinspeople were returning from Hwéeldi.

Amid the growing public criticism, Carleton hastened to assure his superiors that indeed the reservation was succeeding. Carleton sent his orders from Santa Fe: the irrigation ditches must be extended and individual Navajo families should have land allocated to them along the irrigation ditches. He went on to write, "The garrison at Sumner must realize the value of the overall program both to the Indians and to civilization, and give a hand in plowing, planting, and enlarging the ditches."[54] In reality, the reservation was so overburdened with the costs of maintenance, that Carleton told the commanders at Forts Defiance and Wingate that they must

In 1865, Wisconsin senator James Rood Doolittle was appointed chairman of the Doolittle Commission to assess the condition of the western Indian tribes. Doolittle and his colleagues found that the Navajos were not better off at Bosque Redondo, which helped pave the way for their return to their homeland.

keep the prisoners who were waiting to make the journey to Bosque Redondo. By April 1865, more than 9,026 Indians, the majority being Navajos, were at the reservation.

The Doolittle Commission, which was established in 1865 to study the conditions of native peoples in the United States, reached New Mexico in late June 1865 to investigate the reservation and the treatment of natives by civil and military authorities. Spurred by reports of corruption in the Office of Indian Affairs, and especially rumors that the War Department deliberately instigated wars with Indians in order to increase appropriations to the military, Senator James Doolittle took a group of public officials to New Mexico in order to assess the conditions of native peoples, including the Navajos and Mescaleros at Fort Sumner. The final report, known as the Doolittle Report, was published in January 1867. The report noted that Navajos at the fort had not improved their lives at the reservation. While there was little done to address the captives' suffering, the report was important in paving the way for the Navajos' eventual return to their homeland.

THE END OF BOSQUE REDONDO

By 1866, Carleton was relieved of his command in New Mexico. "Fair Carletonia," as Fort Sumner's critics called it, became a casualty of sustained public criticism, mismanagement, and season after season of harsh weather. In addition, the captives continually longing for their homeland, added to the clamor that would undo Carleton's grand scheme. Whenever federal officials visited the fort, Navajo men and women besieged them, clutching at them and pleading that they should be allowed to return to their homeland. Navajo stories indicate that they often took matters into their own hands. As the time and the situation demanded, they acted to ensure their survival. Many stories tell of how the medicine people conducted a ceremony, Ma'ii' Bizéé'nast'á (Put

Bead in Coyote's Mouth), to prophesize about their future as a people. According to Navajo Fred Descheene, the Diné said, "We are lonesome for our land. How can we return to it?"[55] Suffering greatly and longing for their homeland, the medicine men conducted Ma'ii' Bizéé'nast'á by capturing a coyote and placing a bead in its mouth. The medicine men interpreted the coyote's actions, saying that the People would return to Dinétah before too long.

By 1867, the Diné were losing heart and threatening to rebel. In August of that year, a fight broke out between the Navajo men and the U.S. soldiers. According to Navajo leaders, a misunderstanding between Navajo warriors and the soldiers led to bloodshed when the Navajos thought the soldiers wanted to fight them. Manuelito and Barboncito explained that the incident was not meant to happen and that only a few of the Navajo men had been involved. The matter was resolved peacefully, but it was only one of several that occurred at the reservation. In the spring of 1868, federal officials finally conceded that Bosque Redondo had failed.

The next question was, "Where would the Navajos go?" On May 28, 1868, General William Sherman and Samuel Tappan, both of whom had been appointed to the Indian Peace Commission by President Andrew Johnson the previous year, met with Navajo leaders to discuss the condition of their people. A council convened and Barboncito was called upon by his people to speak on their behalf, to negotiate what would be the last treaty the Diné would sign with the United States. Chosen for his eloquence, Barboncito described the harsh realities of exile and captivity and his people's hopes and desires for a future of peace and prosperity. "I cannot rest comfortable at night. I am ashamed to go to the Commissary for my food, it looks as if somebody was waiting to give it to me since the time I was very small until I was a man when

I had my father and mother to take care of,"[56] he said of the dire conditions the Navajos faced. The leader asserted with much dignity, "Our Grandfathers had no idea of living in any other country except our own." He continued, "It was told to us by our forefathers, that we were never to move east of the Rio Grande or west of the San Juan rivers and I think that our coming here has been the cause of so much death among us and our animals." He explained that they had endeavored to make the best of their situation but the land did not know them: "This ground we were brought here we have done all we could possibly do, but found it to be labor in vain, and have therefore quit it. For that reason we have not planted or tried to do anything this year." Of his people's poverty, he said, "The Commissioners can see themselves that we have hardly any sheep or horses, nearly all that we brought here have died and that has left us so poor that we have no means wherewith to buy others."[57]

Of course, Barboncito brought up the question of when the Diné would have their women and children, who had been held captive in New Mexican households, returned to them. Sherman agreed to look into the matter, saying, "We will do all we can to have your children returned to you. Our government is determined that the enslavement of the Navajoes shall cease and those who are guilty of holding them as peons shall be punished."[58]

General Sherman then spoke and said that he was persuaded by the Diné leader's words and added, "You are right, the world is big enough for all the people it contains and all should live at peace with their neighbors."[59] Next, Sherman suggested the possibility of removing the Navajos to Indian Territory. Barboncito's reply was firm: "I hope to God you will not ask me to go to any other country except my own."

Sherman found the Navajo leader's arguments persuasive and agreed to allow the Navajos to return to their land.

Although General William Tecumseh Sherman planned to relocate the Navajos to a reservation in Kansas or Indian Territory after Bosque Redondo had been deemed a failure, he was persuaded by Barboncito to let the Navajos return to their traditional homeland. On June 1, 1868, Sherman and 29 Navajo headmen, including Barboncito, Armijo, Manuelito, Ganado Mucho, and Delgarito, signed the peace treaty that enabled the Navajos to return home.

With the proceedings having ended favorably for the Navajos, Barboncito was thankful and declared, "After we get back to our country, it will brighten up again and Navajos will be as happy as the land. Black clouds will rise and there will be plenty of rain. Corn will grow in abundance and everything will look happy."[60] On May 30, the council ended and a treaty was drafted.

Adding to the earnest pleas of the Navajos that they be allowed to return home, Indian agent Theodore Dodd drafted a report on the status of the Navajos at the reservation, observing he was "satisfied the Navajos will never be contented to remain on this or any other reservation except one located west of the Rio Grande." He went on to declare, "I am also of the opinion that if they are not permitted to return to their old country that many will stealthily return and in doing so commit depredations upon the people of N.M. and thus keep up a state of insecurity."[61]

The treaty between the United States and the Navajos was signed on June 1, 1868. Barboncito and Manuelito were among the signatories of the document. Among the treaty provisions were stipulations about land base, American education for children, instruction in Christianity, and annuities for 10 years. The Navajo leaders also agreed to allow the establishment of trading posts in their country and not to object if a railroad was constructed in their territory. Francis Toledo, a Navajo who witnessed the agreements between the United States and his people, remembered that the peace commissioner asked the Diné "if they would set down their bows and arrows." They answered in the affirmative. Next the People were asked, "Are you going to let your children go to school?"[62] Upon the conclusion of the treaty negotiations and the proclamation made that they would return to their beloved homeland, Manuelito said, "The days and nights were long before it came time for us to go to our homes . . . When we saw the top of the mountain from Albuquerque we wondered if it was our mountain, and we felt like talking to the ground, we loved it so, and some of the old men and women cried with joy when they reached their homes."[63] Years later, in 1966, Manuelito's last surviving son, Naltsoos Neiyéhí (Mail Carrier), who was by then an elder, remembered that his father wished fervently that his people would always remember that the Diné had endured so that the coming generations would remember the importance of 'Iiná, or Life. Manuelito had said, "Life does not end. It goes on."[64] Today, the treaty testifies to the sovereignty of the Navajo Nation and that the United States recognizes the Navajos' sovereignty. The treaty is also a reminder to the Diné of how their grandmothers and grandfathers had courageously challenged American expansion, and survived the war against them, so that future generations could prosper.

Even though the Navajos returned to only a portion of the land they had once inhabited, they were still joyful. Seventeen days later, on June 18, more than 8,000 Diné began the journey home. The caravan extended for at least 10 miles. Just as most had walked to Bosque Redondo, they again walked on the trip home. Fifty-six wagons carried the elders, the ill, and the young. Although they only had 940 sheep, 1,025 goats, and 1,550 horses amongst them, it would not be long before their herds began to prosper. Once they passed Albuquerque and the Rio Grande, they recognized their sacred Tsoo dzil, or Mount Taylor, near present-day Grants, New Mexico, and they cried with joy and thanked the Holy People for answering their prayers. They were almost home.

The Navajos returned too late in the season to plant crops. Instead, in addition to annuities provided under the treaty, they were forced to rely on rations, wild foods, and the help of some Navajos who had maintained herds in the farthest reaches of their lands. Upon their return home, they conducted cleansing ceremonies, to remove the taint of the foreign from their spirits, minds, and bodies. They

THE TREATY OF 1868 (NAAŁ TSOOS SÁNÍ)

On June 1, 1868, Diné leaders signed what would be the last treaty with the United States. For Diné, the immediate significance of the treaty meant the end of four long years of hardship and suffering at a foreign place and a return to their homeland. Politically and culturally, the treaty is an acknowledgement of Navajo sovereignty. Since their ancestors' return from Hwéeldi, Navajo leaders continue to expect the United States to uphold the provisions set forth in the 1868 treaty, which was only one of two agreements between Navajos and the U.S. ratified by Congress. Navajos also take time to celebrate the signing of the treaty with celebrations held every June, the month when the treaty was signed in 1868.

Prior to the treaty of 1868, Navajo leaders had signed treaties with Spain and then with Mexico. These agreements were intended to keep the peace, create alliances, allow trade, and the exchange of captives. Navajo leaders signed a total of nine treaties with the United States, of which Congress only ratified two. The first was ratified in 1849. Like the agreements signed with Spain and Mexico, the treaties of 1849 and 1868 had provisions for peace, trade, and the exchange of captives that both Nations held. The 1868 treaty included provisions such as the delivery of annuities to Navajos for a period of 10 years, American education for Navajo children, and the replacement of livestock lost during their internment as Bosque Redondo. The treaty also established the boundaries of the Navajo reservation, which contained only a fourth of the land that Navajos had formerly claimed. However, a number of executive orders expanded Navajo land boundaries into the 1930s. Today, Diné Békayah is approximately 17.3 million acres and includes land in the states of Arizona, New Mexico, and Utah.

The 1868 treaty remains an important document that symbolizes Navajo sovereignty and the contract that Diné leaders made

(continues)

(continued)

with the U.S. government. Over the decades, Navajos and their leaders have celebrated the signing of the treaty to remind their citizens about the trust relationship between the Navajo Nation and the United States and to proclaim the continuing need to preserve cultural values and traditions. In 1998, the Friends of the Navajo Treaty Project, under the direction of Navajo scholars Evangeline Parsons-Yazzie and Joe Kee, brought the original treaty from the National Archives in Washington, D.C., for a yearlong display at Northern Arizona University in Flagstaff.

Over the course of the year, thousands of Navajos traveled to Flagstaff to view the sacred document. Known as "Naał Tsoos Sání," to Navajos, the treaty was accompanied by a photograph exhibition that showed Navajo life at Fort Sumner in the 1860s. For the Navajo people, the exhibit served as a reminder of the collective experiences of their ancestors who had suffered extreme deprivations when they were forcibly relocated to a strange place more than 350 miles from their homeland. The treaty allowed them moments to send prayers to the Holy People, their ancestors, and their leaders who had shed their blood in order to keep their land and their freedom. On June 1, 1999, the Friends of the Treaty Project celebrated Navajo sovereignty with day-long events that included speakers such as Navajo Nation president Kelsey Begay, Joe Kee, and Navajo poet Laura Tohe. The farewell to the treaty honored the Navajos who had survived Hwéeldi and called for Navajos to continue to preserve the sovereignty of their nation.

then conducted Blessingway ceremonies, for they returned to Hózhó, the path to Beauty and Old Age. The leaders also conducted ceremonies to reestablish Navajo leadership for the people. Today, the People look to the future; at the same time, they have not forgotten their ancestors' ordeals during the Long Walk and their time at Bosque Redondo. They honor their leaders, and their grandmothers and grandfathers, for surviving the horrors of military defeat, removal, and relocation.

Remembering the Long Walk and Hwéeldi

GUS BIGHORSE, ONE OF THE WARRIORS WHO RODE WITH Manuelito during those dark years of the Long Walk and the time at Bosque Redondo, or Hwéeldi, as it is known in Navajo, lived well into the twentieth century and relayed the stories of his life and the Diné to his daughter Tiana who then wrote them down. In his remembrances, the elder expressed the importance of commemorating these narratives to his daughter, saying, "Someday it will be the end of my journey, but I've had a long life, and I will live through my children and my grandchildren and my great-grandchildren and even three times great-grandchildren."[65]

Bighorse's fervent hope that the Diné remember the sacrifices of their ancestors has borne fruit, for indeed several generations later, they have taken these accounts and created an impressive body of stories, songs, poetry, and art that illustrates the impact of this seminal moment and its shaping of Diné identity, culture, and politics. In the decades after the return to their homeland, the Diné endeavored to reestablish their lives based on the philosophy of Hózhó. Throughout

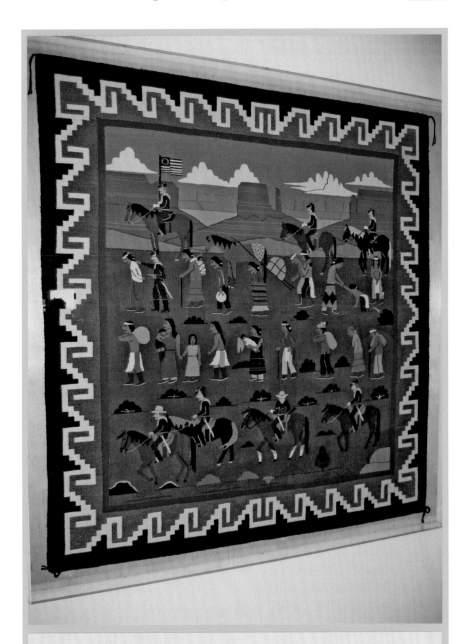

For Navajos, the Long Walk is a seminal moment in history, and the sacrifices made by their ancestors will never be forgotten. This Navajo rug depicts the Long Walk and was on display at the Bosque Redondo Memorial in Fort Sumner, New Mexico for the official opening on June 4, 2005.

the early years of life on the Navajo reservation, the stories of the Long Walk were preserved, and in the 1950s, when the process for the land claims began, the narratives became available in public forums. In particular, with the centennial anniversary of the return from Bosque Redondo in 1968, the ancestors' experiences were rearticulated to strengthen a collective Navajo identity and nationalism. Additionally, Diné scholars, educators, poets, performance artists, and professional storytellers have contributed significantly toward the remembrance of their ancestors' sacrifices. These works commemorate those dark times, bear witness to the horrors that their ancestors endured, and, in the process, also honor grandmothers and grandfathers for their courage and perseverance. The remembrances also offer proof of the value of the traditional Navajo worldview, for it has been Diné philosophy, ceremonies, and prayers that have ensured the survival and revitalization of the People.

REESTABLISHING THEMSELVES

Many Navajo stories begin with the ancestors' return from Hwéeldi. With the signing of the 1868 treaty, the United States acknowledged Navajo claims to a portion of their former homelands; more importantly, for Navajos, the treaty also meant the reestablishment of their homes based on the Diné philosophy Sa' ah naagháí bik'eh hózhóón and the establishment of a government based on self-determination. According to traditional stories, the song "Shí Naashá" was composed to commemorate the return home. The song's title translates as "I Am Going" and the lyrics, both in Navajo and English, are as follows:

> Ahala ahalágó naashá gha I am going in freedom
> Shí naashá gha, shí naashá gha I am going in beauty all around me.
> Shí naashá lago hózhóó ghá I am

Shí naashá gha, shí naashá gha I am going, I am going in beauty;
shí naashá, ládéé hózhóó lá It is around me.[66]

The song conjures images of the People moving and getting ready to make the return home: Mothers and grandmothers preparing bedding, clothing, and foodstuffs for the move; children running about, caught up in the excitement; fathers and grandfathers checking horses and livestock to make sure that all are readied for the long journey. The words, "I am going" is a declaration of being, of saying, "I Am" and "I am a Being." The lyrics reflect how the ancestors overcame the challenge of being forced to live at Hwéeldi to reestablish their lives based on Hózhó. The song is joyful: the ancestors are traveling once again and returning to hózhó, the path of Beauty and Old Age.

Once the People reached their homeland, many went to forts Wingate and Defiance, for they had missed the planting season and had to rely on annuities from the U.S. government. Under the 1868 treaty, the Diné received 15,000 sheep and 500 heads of cattle. Other families did not wait at the forts; they immediately headed back to their former residences. One Diné elder, Betty Shorthair, recalled her ancestors' return: "They walked back to Fort Defiance, and rations were given to them along with one sheep, two sheep or even three sheep." She continued, "They were also given iron hoes, shovels, picks and axes, and they were told to work with those tools on the land they once had."[67] Relatives who had stayed behind welcomed the returning Diné and shared their food and shelter.

RETURNING TO TRADITIONAL WAYS

In the decades after the return and into the 1930s, the People struggled to revitalize their herds. The women resumed weaving textiles. Formerly, they had provided very well for

Raising sheep has long been an important aspect of Navajo culture because sheep embody the principles of K'e, or kinship, and teach industry, responsibility, and trust to all Navajos. Here, a Navajo sheepherder tends a flock near Window Rock, Arizona, in the late 1940s.

their families with their weavings. Now, they saw little economic return for their labor but continued to weave because there were few other avenues to sustain their families. Besides that, weaving was one way that cultural values were practiced and passed on to the next generation. Families also resumed planting their fields, which was also part of the process of revitalizing cultural practices.

In addition, raising livestock was important, because sheep embodied the principles of K'e—kinship—and taught

industry, responsibility, and faith to all Diné. Tending livestock also meant that Navajos had to continually search for
pastureland, which forced some Navajos to use land outside
the Navajo reservation, lands they had formerly controlled.
To meet the Navajos' growing population, the original reservation increased in size several times throughout the early
twentieth century. To ensure the vitality of their herds, Navajos refrained from eating their sheep. Rather, they hunted
deer and antelope for meat and grew corn, squash, water-
melon, and beans. They supplemented these food sources
with piñon nuts and wild plants.

The Diné were so successful in reviving their herds that by
the 1880s, Indian agent Dennis Riordan reported a substan-
tial increase in their numbers. However, at the same time,
Riordan was alarmed at the environmental damage to the
land—it seemed that there was overgrazing, which, in turn,
created widespread gullying, or soil runoff. Riordan called
for livestock reduction by at least one-half to two-thirds. By
1933, Navajos owned more than 1 million head of livestock,
the majority being sheep and goats, but, once again, they
felt the iron fist of the federal government when they were
ordered to reduce their vast flocks and herds.[68]

Under Office of Indian Affairs commissioner John Collier,
the livestock reduction mandates went into effect. This new
threat to their pastoral way of life resulted in Navajos seeking
wage jobs off the reservation, for few jobs existed within their
homeland. At the same time that Navajos were experiencing
such turmoil, they were expected to support the Indian Reorganization Act of 1934 (IRA), legislation that would allow
Native Americans more control over their political, economic, and social lives. Due to the fact that it was introduced
at the same time as forced livestock reduction, Navajo leaders rejected the measures, much to Collier's disappointment.
Nevertheless, a tribal government formulated on IRA guide-
lines was established in 1937. Thus, the IRA paved the way

for the modern Navajo government. During the Red Power movement of the late 1960s, Navajo leaders affirmed Navajo sovereignty and the right to self-government.[69]

SOVEREIGNTY

In 1968, to mark Navajo sovereignty, chairman Raymond Nakai announced the observation of the one-hundredth, or centennial, anniversary of the return from Bosque Redondo with cultural events over the course of that year. Events included essay contests for students, a fair, a re-enactment of the return from Fort Sumner and the signing of the treaty of 1868, and several publications that included books, photographs, and a giant calendar. Throughout the year, the *Navajo Times* regularly published articles and documents from the mid-nineteenth century; while most of these were non-Navajo sources, oral histories were included. Gauging how far the Navajos had come since the events of 1863 to 1868, Navajo leaders declared the establishment of the modern Navajo government as a way to mark the successful Navajo entrance into American society. In his speech delivered at the opening of the centennial year, Nakai summed up the meaning of the anniversary, saying that for the Navajo people, it had not been an easy time. He noted that Navajos had always fought for a better way of life, "All in all, this past one hundred years does reflect great progress on the part of our people."[70] Integral to interpretations of the birth of the modern Navajo Nation is the idea of "progress," which suggests that Navajos have retained cultural continuity with the past and, at the same time, successfully adapted American values and practices to their way of life.

The treaty of 1868 has played a significant role in the establishment of the modern Navajo Nation, and in the years since, it would be central in affirming Navajo sovereignty.

(continues on page 106)

FROM TRADITIONAL DINÉ GOVERNMENT TO THE NAVAJO NATION

Prior to Euro-American invasion, the Diné were an autonomous people who became wealthy when sheep and horses were integrated into their society beginning in the eighteenth century. Diné autonomy extended to their economic system, which included the trade of the textiles that women wove, and a system of government based on traditional principles of governance. After 1868, with the beginning of the reservation period, Navajos were exposed to American forms of governance that have almost completely undermined traditional forms. However, today, Diné leaders and citizens are considering a return to a traditional form of governance.

During the time of the Long Walk and the years at Hwéeldi, Navajos experienced vast transformations of their political system that have continued to the present day. First, the traditional Navajo political entity, known as a *natural community* by anthropologists, was composed of local bands that consisted of 10 to 40 families. In the largest assembly, called a *naachid*, which was a regional gathering, 24 headmen, 12 of whom were peace leaders and 12 of whom were war leaders, met to address internal matters, intertribal affairs, hunting, and food gathering. During years of peace the peace leader presided, and during wartime the war leader presided. Navajo political organization did not extend beyond local bands, which were led by *Naataanii*, or leaders. Although leaders were men who were referred to as headmen, or chiefs, women could be a Naataanii. The Diné political process was closely tied to their ceremonial life, and the naachid functioned to cure individuals, to bring rain, and to restore the fertility of the soil. The last naachid was reportedly held around 1858, prior to the attack on Fort Defiance led by Manuelito and Barboncito. At this last naachid, Manuelito successfully

(continues)

(continued)

persuaded his people that war with the Americans was the only way to stop the invasions into their country.

Headmen were made leaders based on their own abilities to serve the people. They were expected to ensure proper behavior, maintain moral injunction such as prohibitions against incest and adultery, and enforce economic laws. Often medicine men themselves, headmen served as intermediaries between the People and the Holy People. They relied upon the *hastói* (elder men) and the *hataali* (medicine people) for guidance. After a natural community selected a headman, he went through an initiation process that included a Blessingway. The initiation included the anointing of the new leader's lips with corn pollen.

While it was rare for women to become leaders, early American accounts have noted Navajo women's presence in council proceedings between Navajo and American leaders. As the Navajo educator Ruth Roessel has noted, Navajo women were not appointed as leaders of natural communities but they influenced the decisions that male leaders made on behalf of their people. Certainly, the wife of Manuelito, who is known in historical and oral accounts as Juanita, and Asdzáá Tł'ógi by Navajos, was respected as an influential leader among her people and was known to counsel her husband.

During the Spanish and Mexican periods, the Diné maintained their autonomy. However, with the American invasion in 1846, Navajos found it increasingly difficult to practice their way of life, including their political system, particularly because slave raiders targeted Navajo women and children, which led to cycles of peace and hostilities between Navajos, New Mexicans, and Americans. In 1863, Navajos experienced dramatic transformations during Kit Carson's burn and scorch campaign, after which thousands were sent to Bosque Redondo.

After four long years of suffering at Bosque Redondo, Navajo leaders negotiated a treaty with the United States that allowed them to return to their beloved homeland. The experience at Bosque Redondo dramatically transformed the Navajo political system. For example, the naachid was no longer performed. However, upon their return to their homeland, Navajo leaders conducted a ceremony to reaffirm the chiefs' roles as leaders of the People. Led by their leaders, the People went to Window Rock, where a Blessingway was performed, sacred mountain soil bundles were tied, and each headman took a bundle and passed through Window Rock four times.

The signing of the 1868 treaty proved to be advantageous for the Navajo people when we consider that so many other native peoples were dispossessed of their lands and relocated to Indian Territory in Oklahoma. Over the decades, Navajos remembered the significance of the treaty of 1868, especially as they sought to exercise their rights as a sovereign nation. In the 1920s, the U.S. government created the first Navajo "business" council for the express purpose of expediting tribal business with oil and natural gas companies eager to drill on Dinétah. The establishment of this council was part of the American assimilation process that emphasized patriarchical values. Henry Chee Dodge, Charlie Mitchell, and Da'gha Chii Bik'is were appointed to this first council in 1922. Early council meetings were convened under the direction of the Commissioner to the Navajos, Herbert Hagerman, who had the final word in all council proceedings.

In the 1930s and 1940s, alongside forced livestock reduction mandates, Navajos were expected to accept the Indian Reorganization Act (IRA). Although many have seen the IRA as beneficial because it halted land allotment and brought self-governance, Navajos rejected the act because they linked it to livestock reduction, much to the disappointment of Office of Indian Affairs Commissioner

(continues)

(continued)

John Collier. Although Navajo leaders rejected the IRA, Navajos were subjected to government rule based on Western democratic principles. In 1938, the Navajo Tribal Council was reorganized and later, in 1989, renamed the Navajo Nation Council. Today, this IRA model still informs the contemporary Navajo Nation government with its three branches of government, the legislative, executive, and judicial.

In 1968, Navajo leaders staged a number of cultural events to celebrate Navajo "progress," including the reenactment of the return from Bosque Redondo and the re-signing of the Treaty of 1868, which were designed to promote Navajo identity. In 1969, the Navajo Tribal Council officially changed the Navajo polity from "the Navajo Tribe" to "the Navajo Nation." This change reflected Navajo determination to exercise their collective rights to territory and sovereignty.

Today, the Navajo Nation operates under a government created by well-meaning U.S. federal officials and struggles to claim its sovereignty in every sense of the word. Like other Indian governments, the Navajo Nation has experienced political turmoil that pitted tribal members against each other and threatened to tear communities apart. While a number of reforms, like Title II, have been designed to check the abuse of power and to bring in traditional forms of governance, except for the peacemaker's court, there are few traditional elements of government evident in the present-day Navajo political structure. However, Navajo leaders do continue to rely on traditional ceremonies for affirmation and guidance; though, in many cases, these rituals are performed within their personal and kin networks.

(continued from page 102)

In 1968, the commemoration celebrations emphasized the United States' recognition of Navajo sovereignty and, importantly, the treaty's facilitation of the Navajos' return to their homeland. As historian Peter Iverson observed of this momentous occasion, "Now, through the treaty of 1868, they [Navajos] would be returned to a portion of their old home country, but they would return to a reservation with strictly defined borders. Their political boundaries had been established: the Navajo Nation had begun."[71] The image of a people surviving against incredible odds is a common theme in American history. According to this type of narrative, the Diné, like other peoples, had survived an ordeal in their history and emerged as citizens of a new nation.

REMEMBRANCE

Alongside the birth of the newly constituted Navajo Nation, a host of Navajo educators, scholars, poets, writers, and performance artists, some riding the currents of Red Power to revitalize and claim cultural values and traditions, disseminated the stories of their ancestors in mediums that ranged from songs to prose and poetry to art. One of the most prominent poets, Luci Tapaphonso, created "In 1868," a poem that echoes the themes and imagery associated with oral tradition. In this poem, the narrator is driving near Fort Sumner when she realizes how the land she is crossing is connected to the stories of the ancestors she had heard about as a child. It is here that her ancestors had eked out a living. The narrator tells a story of a Navajo man who was working near Hwéeldi and found that it distressed him to be at the place where his ancestors had suffered so greatly. In response to the ancestors' "cries and moans carried by the wind and blowing snow," he prayed and sang for them. The sounds of anguish made him wonder how his own family was faring in his absence, and he eventually quits his job and makes his way home. The narrator then shifts the story to the ancestors' trials, and the listeners are overcome with grief when they hear about what they had to overcome. She informs her audience that the People had met hardships with faith, "We will be strong as long as we are together," and that prayers to the Holy People had fortified their ancestors. Likewise, in the present, they still call upon the Holy People for fortification.

Poet and educator Rex Lee Jim also shares how the Long Walk has shaped his identity as a Diné man. In "A Moment in Time," Jim indicates how Western education had alienated him from his traditional values but that he had reclaimed them after a period. Explaining how traditional ceremonies and stories had sustained the grandparents during the Long Walk, Jim gets down on his knees and pretends to pick undigested corn kernels out of horse manure, in much the same manner that the captives had during the forced march.[72] The starving prisoners had appeased their hunger pangs in any possible manner. Jim's performance explains to his students the depths of the humiliation and debasement that Navajo people had been driven to in order to survive. Examples of the duress that the ancestors experienced will perhaps bring about an appreciation for the People's determination to retain their lands and cultural integrity.

Music is another form of remembrance that honors the Long Walk. Drawing upon traditional forms of Navajo music, artists such as Marilyn Help Hood, Radmilla Cody, and Jay Begay have composed songs that recall the historical experiences of their ancestors during the nineteenth century. Marilyn Help Hood is a former Miss Navajo who is today a Navajo cultural teacher at Wingate Elementary School, where she teaches Navajo studies. In her coauthored book, *We'll Be in Your Mountains, We'll Be in Your Songs*, Help explains how she was taught about Navajo culture during her childhood, which helped her win the Miss Navajo title as a young woman. Among other songs, Help also performs "Shí Naashá," which she believes has an important meaning: "The words in the song mean that you have a feeling for yourself that you are going to survive, that you are special, and that you are going to live a long life."[73]

Like the song "Shí Naashá," Radmilla Cody's "The Return Home" is also a song of renewal and celebration. Based on the stanza from the Blessingway prayers, this composition links the journeys that Navajos have made to their determination during their imprisonment and afterwards to follow the path of Beauty and Old Age. Cody's song tells us that, upon their return, the grandmothers and grandfathers immediately reestablished their lives based on hózhó. Their prayers to the Holy People embodied their thankfulness for their land, home, and kin relationships, and that hózhó would once again serve as the template for their lives.

In pointing out the significance of the Long Walk and how the experience is tied to the present for Navajos, Cody says, "Our forbearers were overwhelmed with emotion and elation when they returned home from the Long Walk. We feel it today when we return home from our travels.[74]

Navajo performer Jay Begay's composition "Hwéeldi Chill" combines traditional forms with flute music. The song begins with a fiery sounding thunderstorm that brings hard rains but in the end yields harvest, for the earth and all living beings are dependent upon the rains that come after the thunderstorms for life. Thunderstorms bring life-giving rains. Begay's song imparts the lessons learned from the Long Walk—that Navajos have endured incredible hardship, but that they have learned to always look to the future, to be hopeful for better times. He stresses that prayers were crucial to the ancestors' survival. Begay's song reminds Navajos that it was the prayers and traditions that carried the People through such harsh times. He writes, "Keep tradition strong."[75]

New songs about the Long Walk also reflect changes that Navajos have embraced. In particular, "Blood, Sweat, and Tears," by Johnny Mike and Verdell Primeaux, illustrate the range of mediums that are used to teach and remind Navajos about what happened in the nineteenth century.[76] The

In 2002, Verdell Primeaux (left) and Johnny Mike (right) won a Grammy Award for best Native American Music Album for *Bless the People—Harmonized Peyote Songs*. The duo would later record "Blood, Sweat, and Tears," which recounts the Navajos' experience during the Long Walk.

peyote religion, also known as the Native American Church of North America (NAC), swept through the Navajo homeland in the 1930s during the period of livestock reduction. The songs that accompany prayers during the night-long NAC prayer meeting are usually only sung for the purpose of the church; however, artists like Mike and Primeaux have expanded the repertoire of NAC music by harmonizing with the flute and other instruments and by popularizing the form by referencing Navajo experiences like the Long Walk. In "Blood, Sweat, and Tears," the sound is melancholy and Mike and Primeaux acknowledge the nightmare that this experience was for the Navajo people. These NAC members' composition also illustrates how Navajos have embraced some elements of Christianity, which the peyote religion has incorporated. Simultaneously, the song's lyrics urge parents and grandparents to teach children traditional values and remind them that it is these same values that helped the ancestors get through the Long Walk and Hwéeldi.

MEMORIALIZING THE LONG WALK AND HWÉELDI

The significance of the treaty of 1868 as both a document of Navajo sovereignty and a vehicle to foster a collective Navajo identity remained important at the end of the twentieth century. On June 1, 1999, another recognition of Navajo nationhood took place when hundreds of Diné and their supporters gathered at Northern Arizona University in Flagstaff, Arizona, to celebrate Treaty Day, a day Navajo leaders set aside to commemorate the treaty signed in 1868 between Navajo leaders and Americans. The treaty was flown from the National Archives in Washington, D.C., to Flagstaff, Arizona, where thousands of Navajos viewed the document. Sight of the treaty unleashed a flood of stories passed down through Diné memory. While the People remember the nightmare of the 1860s, when Americans subjugated their ancestors, they also tell stories of how their ancestors had made sacrifices so that the Navajos could return to their beloved homeland and begin the process of rebuilding their lives.

In New Mexico, beginning in 1992, both Navajo and non-Navajo organizations combined their efforts to establish a state memorial dedicated to the Navajos' experiences during the period of American expansion. The New Mexico state legislature passed a bill requesting that the Office of Cultural Affairs continue the efforts to establish Bosque Redondo as a memorial to the Navajo people. With state monies, a building would be established to house a museum and visitor center. Although the Office of Cultural Affairs sought to include Navajos in the planning stages of the memorial, many Navajos were concerned about the interpretations that would be offered at the site. Many realized that Navajos often had a different and even contradictory perspective on the meaning of the Long Walk and Hwéeldi. For example, Jose Cisneros and Gregory Scott Smith acknowledged the importance of the memorial, by declaring: "It will honor the memory of thousands of Navajo and Mescalero Apache people who suffered and died as a result of the forced relocation and internment. Moreover, it will celebrate the official birth of a sovereign nation born of the tragedy of Bosque Redondo."[77] The comparison of the memorial to others throughout the world that honor and preserve memories of similar tragedies acknowledges the wrongs perpetrated by the United States against its original inhabitants.

In the further effort to move toward creating the memorial, in November 2005, the National Park Service held a conference in Window Rock, Arizona, to invite Navajo input to the proposal to create the memorial. The People still remember those dark years with pain and bitterness. A day of testimony about the Long Walk and Hwéeldi made it clear that the years have had little effect on the impact those events have had on the Navajo consciousness. Waiting patiently all

Opened in June 2005, the Bosque Redondo Memorial is located in east-central New Mexico, approximately 160 miles east of Albuquerque. Pictured here is the entrance to memorial, which was designed by Navajo architect David Sloan.

day and listening to speakers who explained the importance of establishing the memorial, local community members finally got a chance to share their stories. Just as their grandparents had heard the stories and conveyed them to the next generation, the participants shared their stories, which were filled with brutal images of violence, hunger, sickness, and loneliness. At various times throughout the day, there were many moments where emotions threatened to overcome the presenters and the audience alike. While Navajo stories do not hold back in their depiction of the inhumanity shown to the People, they have also become part of the movement toward healing and reconciliation.

The establishment of the proposed memorials also sparked debate between Navajos and non-Navajos. On the one hand, the memorial was intended to remind Americans of significant Native American events but also to remind Americans of the injustices that Navajos and other Native Americans were forced to endure at the hands of the U.S. government. Some Navajos were also skeptical because they believed that many non-Indians preferred a sanitized version of American history, where the dispossession of native peoples and the brutality they experienced is not addressed. For example, in a 1980 publication, historian David Lavender wrote that Navajos had benefited from their years at Bosque Redondo because they had gained "an improved knowledge of agriculture and vocational trades, better methods of constructing the hogans in which they lived, and an appreciation of the wagon." According to Lavender, "The people as a whole had a fresh, strong sense of the tribal unity, and a determination somehow to make their way peacefully in the Anglo worlds while retaining their own values."[78] For non-Indian historians then, the Bosque Redondo experience not only transformed Navajos into model American citizens who realized the benefits of white civilization, but for Navajos, the series of events were the catalyst that established the foundation for the modern Navajo Nation.

In another example, in 1998, in an update of his study on Navajos at Bosque Redondo, historian Lynn Bailey delivered an interpretation similar to that of Lavender. According to Bailey, during the years the United States fought the Navajos, the Navajos had a "choice" of either retreating farther into the homeland or surrendering and marching to the Fort Sumner internment camp. The "choice" to endure the prison camp was "not entirely without benefit."[79] During their internment at the camp, Navajos exhibited some art at farming, and the "irrigation system they constructed was probably the most intricate and best engineered in all of New Mexico." They acquired new technologies, replacing the digging stick with hoes, shovels, rakes, and plows. They learned of metal work to make nails, horse and mule shoes, and of course, jewelry. One Navajo man acquired headman status after he demonstrated skill at forging iron.[80]

One of the more public displays of the tension between Navajos and non-Navajos revolves around Christopher "Kit" Carson, who was responsible for the military campaign against the Navajos that ultimately broke their resistance and led to their defeat and removal from their homeland. While Navajos have expressed their disdain for Carson for his role in carrying out the brutal campaign against their kinspeople, which resulted in thousands of deaths, including women, children, and elders, American scholars have named him as either an unsung or reluctant hero. In 2002, Navajo lawmakers, led by New Mexico senator Leonard Tsosie, successfully derailed efforts to declare Carson's Taos home and a museum dedicated to his memory a state monument. Tsosie declared, "You know, many of our people are still wounded by this. I don't think we should be recognizing someone who literally killed thousands of New Mexicans and that's what this individual did." Tsosie compared Carson to former Yugoslav president Slobodan Milosevic, who was found guilty of committing war crimes during the war in Croatia, Bosnia, and Kosovo.[81] The opposition to memorializing Kit Carson's home was so widespread that the measure was set aside and has not been since revived.

In a recent essay, historian Paul Hutton hypothesizes why Kit Carson has not been remembered for his heroic deeds as a frontiersman in the same manner as Daniel Boone or William F. Cody. Hutton suggests that scholars sympathetic to Navajo perspectives, including Peter Iverson and Clifford

New Mexico state senator Leonard Tsosie has been vocal in his opposition to making Kit Carson's Taos, New Mexico, home a state monument and museum. Pictured here in 2007, Tsosie resigned his seat in January to become a member of the Navajo Tribal Council.

Trazfer, have had much to do with Carson's nationwide disgrace and disfavor.[82] Hutton believes that Carson has been unfairly portrayed by a generation of scholars who have seen the evils in American expansion. Manifest destiny did not bring with it democracy, freedom, and opportunity to Native Americans but has meant oppression, violence, and disenfranchisement. Moreover, Hutton insists that Carson was not directly responsible for the deaths of more than 2,500 Navajos, and that under his command, only 23 Navajos died.[83] At the same time, in Fort Defiance, Arizona, Navajo community members are considering renaming Kit Carson Drive, which is the main thoroughfare through town. They also have recommended that the Kit Carson Memorial State Park and the cemetery near Taos be renamed.[84]

As is true of other historic sites that are associated with native-white relationships, the memorial site dedicated to commemorating the Navajos' experiences under American colonialism is rife with tension, as Navajos and their allies voice their disagreement over the meaning of the American past. With the exception of a few historical accounts, narratives of the Navajos' experience have consistently justified the conquest and dispossession and deny the horror, violence, and inhumane treatment of the Diné.

The Bosque Redondo Memorial

On June 4, 2005, the day finally arrived; the years of planning, organizing, and securing funding for the Bosque Redondo Memorial finally paid off. Although additional funding is required to complete the memorial site, the memorial was officially opened on June 4.[85] The citizens of Fort Sumner had done their share to establish the memorial. Naming themselves "Friends of the Bosque Redondo," they had deeded a piece of land for the memorial. On the morning of the official ceremony, they had busily set up breakfast for their Navajo friends who had traveled hundreds of miles to take part in the celebration. At noontime, they would host a barbeque for nearly 1,000 visitors.

Earlier in the morning before the crowds began arriving, a small group of Diné had offered their prayers to the Holy People. Navajos from throughout the country arrived to witness the dedication. Among the dignitaries who took part in the dedication were representatives from the Mescalero Apache Nation, New Mexico state representatives and senators, and Navajo council delegates, including speaker of the Navajo Nation council, Lawrence Morgan. Navajo artist Irvin Toddy and writer Evangeline Parsons-Yazzie sold their artwork and books to those people in attendance. Navajos milled about before the program began and greeted neighbors that they had not seen for a while. As the program unfolded, Navajo dignitaries were forthcoming in describing the brutality and injustices that their ancestors had faced during their time at Bosque Redondo. Speaker of the Navajo Nation Council Lawrence Morgan called Fort Sumner a "slaughterhouse." Navajo speakers hoped that Americans had learned something from this horrific time in history, and that it would not be repeated. They noted that the Navajo people, having survived this trauma, had grown stronger. The Navajos' remembrances were a testimony to their vision, courage, and resilience.

Interestingly, as New Mexico senator Pete Domenici delivered his remarks, Nicole Walker, a Diné woman, interrupted him and began addressing the crowd. In memory of her ancestors who had made the long march to Hwéedi, Walker and her family members had started walking to Fort Sumner at 3 A.M. that morning. Her granddaughter carried the Navajo Nation flag for the contingent. Walker's grief, which was reflected in her crying, moved the audience into a silence that was deafening. In the midst of Walker's actions, reporters and photographers rushed to the front to capture her image during this moment of fracture in the "official"

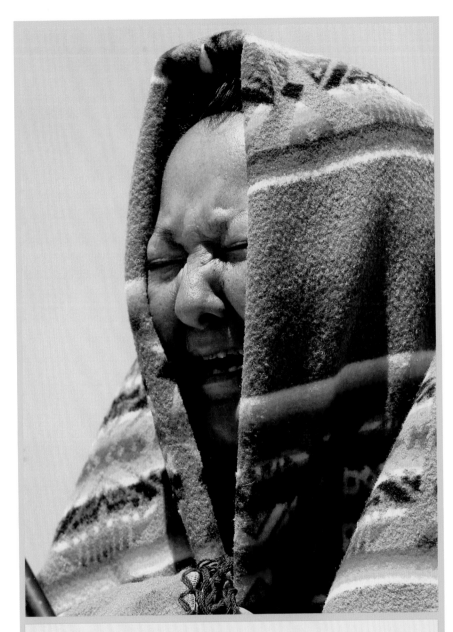

During the dedication ceremonies of the Bosque Redondo Memorial on June 4, 2005, Nicole "Grandma" Walker openly showed the emotions that many Navajos felt that day. Walker and members of her family walked 42 miles from Santa Rosa, New Mexico, to Fort Sumner to attend the event.

program. Certainly, Walker's dramatic performance indicates that the wounds of the Long Walk and Bosque Redondo still run deep. The Navajo people have not allowed non-Navajo interpretations of this important event in their history to be controlled by non-Navajos. They have taken initiatives to ensure that Americans do not forget the unjust treatment of native peoples; however, at the same time, they are determined to rise above the nightmare of the past that continues to haunt them and reclaim the vitality of their cultural inheritance. The stories of the Long Walk and Hwéeldi and what happened to their people has made the Navajos determined to create a better world for the coming generations.

Chronology

A.D. 900–1400 Scholars do not agree on when Navajos migrated into what is now the American Southwest; Navajos say that they emerged into this world from the lower worlds in the area known as the San Juan region of northwestern New Mexico, which they call Dinétah (Navajo Land).

1582 Spaniard Antonio de Espejo becomes first European to encounter the Navajos (in northwestern New Mexico).

1626 Spanish Franciscan friar Zarate Salmeron recognizes the Navajos as a distinct tribe.

1630s–1860s Spanish and later Mexicans carry out slave raids against the Navajos; one of the major reasons for ongoing hostilities between Navajos and their neighbors was directly related to the slave trade, which targeted Navajo women and children; Americans turn a blind eye to the slave trade.

1680 Navajos participate in the Pueblo Revolt, driving Spanish from Pueblo territory.

1706 First peace treaty between Spanish and Navajos.

1749 Spanish establish Catholic missions of Encinal and Cebolleta in Navajo country; some Navajos are exposed to Christianity, but the missionaries are quickly driven out.

1786 At this time, Navajos are divided into five groups: Cayon de Chelly, Cebolleta, Chuska Mountain, Ojo del Oso, and San Mateo.

1821 Mexico declares independence from Spain.

1846   U.S. colonel Stephen Kearny claims Santa Fe, New Mexico, as territorial capital for United States; Navajos and U.S. officials meet at Fort Wingate, New Mexico, to establish peace.

1848   Treaty of Guadalupe Hidalgo ends war between United States and Mexico. Under its terms, more than 1.2 million square miles of territory are ceded by Mexico to the United States for $15 million; The U.S. government claims jurisdiction over all tribal peoples, including Navajos, in the Southwest.

1849   Treaty signed between U.S. government and the Navajos; this treaty along with one

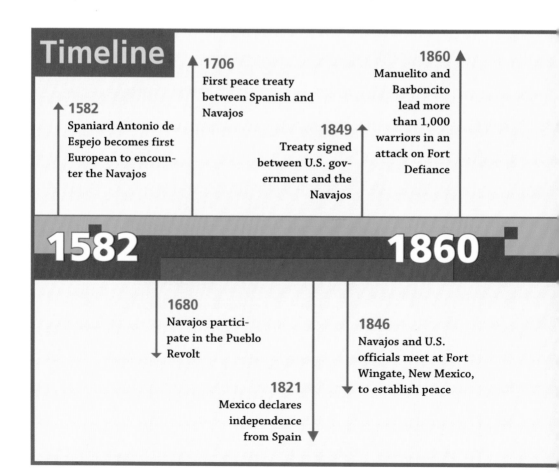

Timeline

1582
Spaniard Antonio de Espejo becomes first European to encounter the Navajos

1706
First peace treaty between Spanish and Navajos

1849
Treaty signed between U.S. government and the Navajos

1860
Manuelito and Barboncito lead more than 1,000 warriors in an attack on Fort Defiance

1582   1860

1680
Navajos participate in the Pueblo Revolt

1821
Mexico declares independence from Spain

1846
Navajos and U.S. officials meet at Fort Wingate, New Mexico, to establish peace

signed in 1868 are the only two of nine signed between the federal government and the Navajos that were ratified by the U.S. Senate.

1855 Manuelito recognized as one of the leading chiefs of the Navajo tribe.

1860 Manuelito and Barboncito lead more than 1,000 warriors in an attack on Fort Defiance in New Mexico Territory.

1863 U.S. government decides to relocate Navajos to an area known as Bosque Redondo (round grove, in Spanish), near Fort Sumner on the Pecos River in what is now east-central New Mexico.

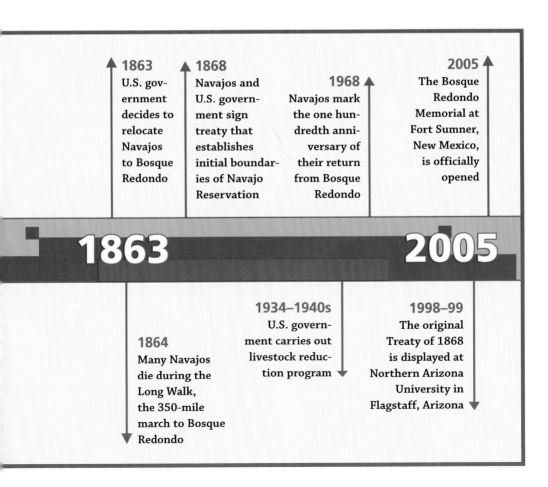

1863 U.S. government decides to relocate Navajos to Bosque Redondo

1868 Navajos and U.S. government sign treaty that establishes initial boundaries of Navajo Reservation

1968 Navajos mark the one hundredth anniversary of their return from Bosque Redondo

2005 The Bosque Redondo Memorial at Fort Sumner, New Mexico, is officially opened

1863

2005

1864 Many Navajos die during the Long Walk, the 350-mile march to Bosque Redondo

1934–1940s U.S. government carries out livestock reduction program

1998–99 The original Treaty of 1868 is displayed at Northern Arizona University in Flagstaff, Arizona

1864 Many Navajos die during the Long Walk, which was actually a series of forced marches—between 350 to 450 miles—to the Navajo reservation at Bosque Redondo.

1866 Manuelito surrenders and many Navajo leaders, including Barboncito, quickly follow suit.

1868 Navajos and U.S. government sign treaty that establishes initial boundaries of Navajo Reservation in northwestern New Mexico (about one-fourth of the tribe's traditional territory); Barboncito was the chief negotiator for the Navajo people.

1878–86 Navajo Reservation is increased in size by five major land annexations; in the 1930s, additional lands are added to the Navajo land base.

1884 Henry Chee Dodge named head chief of the Navajos.

1922 U.S. government creates Navajo Business Council, which includes Chee Dodge, Charlie Mitchell, and Dugal Chee Bekiss; the men are supposed to represent their people in negotiating oil leases with the United States.

1934 Navajos reject Indian Reorganization Act; Congressional legislation adds 243,000 acres of land to Navajo Reservation.

1934–1940s U.S. government carries out livestock reduction program.

1940 Navajos pass resolution banning the use of peyote on reservation lands; Native American Church, which uses the plant in its ceremonies, holds that the resolution violates the First Amendment. In *Native American Church v. Navajo Tribal Council* (1959), federal court holds that First Amendment does not apply to Indian nations.

1968 The Navajo Tribe officially kicks off a year-long remembrance of the one hundredth anniversary of the Navajos' return from Bosque Redondo in 1868.

1969   Navajo Council officially change the name of the Navajo Tribe to the Navajo Nation.

1998–99   The original Treaty of 1868 is displayed at Northern Arizona University in Flagstaff, Arizona, so that Navajos may view the precious document.

2005   The Bosque Redondo Memorial at Fort Sumner, New Mexico, is officially opened on June 4.

2006   Joe Shirley elected to a second term as president of the Navajo Nation.

Notes

Chapter 1

1. Navajos refer to themselves as the Diné, which means the People. Throughout the book, all three terms—*Navajo, Diné,* and *the People*—are used.
2. American Indian and Alaska Native Population 2000. Washington, D.C.: U.S. Census Bureau. 2002. Available online at *http://www.census.gov/prod/2002pubs/c2brol1-15df.*
3. Klara B. Kelley and Harris Francis, "Abalone Shell Buffalo People: Navajo Narrated Routes and Pre-Columbian Archaeological Sites," *New Mexico Historical Review* 78, no. 1 (Winter 2003): 29–58.
4. Robert Young, *The Role of the Navajo in the Southwest Drama* (Gallup, N.M.: Gallup Independent and the Navajo Tribe, 1968), 12–16.
5. David M. Brugge, "Navajo Prehistory and History to 1850," *Handbook of the North American Indians: Southwest*, vol. 10 (Washington, D.C.: Smithsonian Press, 1983); 481–501.

Chapter 2

6. James F. Brooks, *Captives and Cousins: Slavery, Kinship and Community in the Southwest Borderlands* (Chapel Hill: University of North Carolina Press, 2002).
7. Excerpt from Josiah Gregg, *Commerce of the Prairies,* reprinted in J. Lee Correll, *Through White Men's Eyes,* Vol. 1, 182 in Peter Iverson, *Diné: A History of the Navajos* (Albuquerque: University of New Mexico Press, 2002), 33.
8. Frank McNitt, *Navajo Wars: Military Campaigns, Slave Raids, and Reprisals* (Albuquerque: University of New Mexico Press, 1990), 95.
9. Clifford E. Trafzer, *Anglo Expansionists and Navajo Raiders: A Conflict of Interest,* Historical Monograph No. 1, (Tsaile, Ariz.: Navajo Community College Press, 1978), 6.
10. Frank McNitt, *Navajo Wars: Military Campaigns, Slave Raids, and Reprisals*, 118.
11. Jack Utter, "The Death of a Navajo Patriot—And His Ties to Federal Recognition, Treaty Rights, the Trust Relationship, and the San Juan Water Settlement." Unpublished paper in possession of the author, August 3, 2004.
12. McNitt, *Navajo Wars*, 147.
13. Ibid., 319.
14. Brooks to Asst. Adj. General, May 30 and June 25, 1858. Cited in J. Lee Correll, *Through White Men's Eyes,* 129, 130.
15. Ibid., 130–32.
16. Dixon S. Mile, Order no. 3, September 4, 1858. Cited in J. Lee Correll, *Through White Men's Eyes,* 151.

17. Gerald Thompson, *The Army and the Navajo* (Tucson: University of Arizona Press, 1976), 7–9.

18. James Carleton to Thompson, September 19, 1863. Cited in Lawrence C. Kelly, *Navajo Roundup: Selected Correspondence of Kit Carson's Expedition Against the Navajos, 1863–1865* (Boulder, Colo.: Pruett Publishing Co., 1970), 56, 57

19. Carleton to Carson, September 19, 1863. Cited in Kelly, *Navajo Roundup*, 52.

20. Clifford Trazfer, *Kit Carson's Campaign*, 102.

21. Eli Gorman in *Navajo Stories of the Long Walk Period* ed. Broderick H. Johnson (Tsaile: Ariz.: Tsaile Community College Press, 1973): 197–209.

22. Carleton to unnamed addressee, March 21, 1865. Cited in J. Lee Correll, *Through White Men' Eyes*, 92, 93.

23. Tiana Bighorse with Noel Bennett, *Bighorse the Warrior* (Tucson: University of Arizona Press, 1998), 21.

24. Testimony of Dághá Chíí Bi'kis, January 16, 17, 1951, Land Claims Commission Papers, J. Lee Correll Papers, Navajo Nation Library, Window Rock, Ariz.

Chapter 3

25. Luci Tapahonso, "In 1864," *Sáanii Dahataal: The Women are Singing* (Tucson: University of Arizona Press, 1993), 8.

26. Mary Pioche, *Hwéeldi Baa Hané* (1988), 99. Quoted in Neal Ackerley, "A Navajo Diaspora: The Long Walk to Hwéeldi," (Dio Rios Consultants, Inc., 1998). Available online at *http://members.tripod.com/ ~bloodhound/longwalk.htm.* Accessed January 10, 2007.

27. Gus Bighorse quoted in Tiana Bighorse, *Bighorse the Warrior*, 58.

28. Frank Nez, personal conversation, Fort Sumner, New Mexico, April 2005.

29. Chahadineli Benally in *Navajo Stories of the Long Walk*, 57–74.

30. Howard W. Gorman in *Navajo Stories*, 23–42.

31. Frank McNitt, "The Long March: 1863–1867," in *The Changing Ways of Southwestern Indians: A Historic Perspective* ed. Albert H. Schroeder (Glorieta, N.M.: The Rio Grande Press, Inc., 1971), 159.

32. Ibid., 147–48.

33. Ibid., 149.

34. Carleton to Thomas, Feb. 27, 1864. Quoted in J. Lee Correll, *Through White Men's Eyes*, vol. IV, 79, 80.

35. Peshlakai Etsedi, as told to Sallie Pierce Brewer, "The 'Long Walk' to Bosque Redondo," *Navajo Times*, October 17, 1963, 12, 14, 15.

36. Kayah David, quoted in Crawford R. Buell, "The Navajo 'Long Walk': Recollections by Navajos" in *The Changing Ways of Southwestern Indians: A Historic Perspective* ed. Albert H. Schroeder (Glorieta, N.M.: The Rio Grande Press, Inc., 1971), 171.

37. Wardwell report, December 1863, NARA, M1120, Roll 21, Frame 1121. Quoted in Neal Ackerly, "A Navajo Diaspora," 20.

38. John Daw, Testimony before the Land Claims Commission, 1951. Quoted in Crawford R. Buell, "The Navajo 'Long Walk,'" 177.

39. Jeff King, Testimony before the Land Claims Commission, 1951. Quoted in Crawford R. Buell, "The Navajo 'Long Walk,'" 177–79.

40. Capt. Francis McCabe to Asst. Adj. General, May 12, 1864. Reprinted in J. Lee Correll, *Through White Men's Eyes*, 160, 161.

41. McNitt, "The Long March: 1863–1867," 164.

42. *Santa Fe Gazette*, September 29, 1866. Reprinted in Frank McNitt, "The Long March: 1863–1867," 165, 166.

43. Carleton to Major David H. Brotherton, Dec. 21, 1866. Reprinted in J. Lee Correll, *Through White Men's Eyes*, 414.

Chapter 4

44. Gerald Thompson, *The Army and the Navajo* (Tucson: University of Arizona Press, 1976), 19.

45. Robert A. Roessel, Jr., *Pictorial History of the Navajo From 1860 to 1910* (Rough Rock, Ariz.: Navajo Curriculum Center, Rough Rock Demonstration School, 1980).

46. Dugal Tsosie Begay, in *Navajo Stories of the Long Walk*, 213.

47. Ibid., 215.

48. Roseann S. Willink and Paul Zolbrod, *Weaving A World: Textiles and the Navajo Way of Seeing* (Santa Fe: Museum of New Mexico Press, 1996).

49. Thompson, *The Army and the Navajo*, 36.

50. Andrea Smith, *Conquest: Sexual Violence and American Indian Genocide* (Cambridge, Mass.: South End Press, 2005), 55–78.

51. Thompson, *The Army and the Navajo*, 67.

52. Ernest Nelson, in *Navajo Stories of the Long Walk*, 173, 174.

53. Peter Iverson, *Diné: A History of the Navajos* (Albuquerque: University of New Mexico Press, 2002). See also David E. Wilkins, *The Navajo Political Experience* (Tsaile: Ariz.: Diné College Press, 1999).

54. Thompson, *The Army and the Navajo*, 78.

55. Fred Descheene, in *Navajo Stories*, 212.

56. Barboncito, reprinted in *The Navajo Treaty—1868: Treaty Between the United States of America & the Navajo Tribe of Indians/With a Record of the Discussions That led to its Signing* (Las Vegas, Nev.: KC Publications, 1968, 2, 3.

57. Ibid., 2–4.

58. Ibid., 4, 5.

59. Ibid., 4.

60. Ibid., 5, 6.

61. Theo H. Dodd, "Status Report," reprinted in *The Navajo Treaty—1868*, 13–16,

62. Francis Toledo, in *Navajo Stories*, 146, 147.

63. William a. Keleher, *Turmoil in New Mexico, 1846–1868* (Santa

Fe: The Rydal Press, 1952), 277. cited in Crawford R. Buell, "The Navajo 'Long Walk,'" 183.

64. Jennifer Nez Denetdale, *Reclaiming Diné History: The Legacies of Navajo Chief Manuelito and Juanita* (Tucson: University of Arizona Press, 2007), 83.

Chapter 5

65. Tiana Bighorse, *Bighorse the Warrior*, 1.

66. Ellen McCullough–Brabson and Marilyn Help, *We'll Be in Your Mountains, We'll Be in Your Songs: A Navajo Woman Sings* (Albuquerque: University of New Mexico Press, 2001), *65.*

67. Betty Shorthair, *Navajo Stories of the Long Walk Period* ed. Broderick H. Johnson (Tsaile, Ariz.: Navajo Community College Press, 1973): 114, 115.

68. Richard White, *The Roots of Dependency: Subsistence, Environment, and Social Change Among the Choctaws, Pawnees, and Navajos* (Lincoln: University of Nebraska Press, 1983), 212–290.

69. David Wilkins, "Governance within the Navajo Nation: Have Democratic Traditions Taken Hold?" *Wicazo Sa Review* (Spring 2002): vol. 17, no. 1, 91–129.

70. Raymond Nakai, speech delivered at the official opening of the Navajo Centennial year, published in Martin A. Link, ed., *Navajo: 1868–1968: A Century of Progress* (Window Rock, Ariz.: K.C. Publications and the Navajo Tribe, 1968), 108.

71. Peter Iverson, *The Navajo Nation* (Albuquerque: University of New Mexico Press, 1981), 10.

72. Rex Lee Jim, "A Moment in My Life," *Here First: Autobiographical Essays by Native American Writers* ed. Arnold Krupat and Brian Swann (New York: The Modern Library, 2000), 241, 241.

73. Ellen McCullough–Brabson and Marilyn Help, *We'll Be in Your Mountains*, 62,

74. Radmilla Cody, *Seed of Life: Traditional Songs of the Navajo* cd recording, Canyon Records, 2001.

75. Jay Begay and Everitt White, *The Long Walk–Hwééldi*, cd recording, Canyon Records, 1999.

76. Verdell Primeaux and Johnny Mike, "Blood, Sweat, & Tears," *House Before Dawn*, cd recording, Canyon Records, 2002.

77. Ibid., 18.

78. Ibid., 181, 182.

79. Lynn R. Bailey, *Bosque Redondo: The Navajo Internment at Fort Sumner, New Mexico, 1863–68* (Tucson: Westernlore Press, 1998), 197.

80. Ibid., 197–199.

81. Fritz Thompson and Loie Fecteau, "Kit Carson: Hero or Villain?" *Albuquerque Journal* 3 March 2002, A 1.

82. Peter Iverson, *Diné: A History of the Navajos* (Albuquerque: University of New Mexico Press, 2002), xx, and Clifford E. Trafzer, *The Kit Carson Campaign: The Last Great Navajo War* (Norman: University of Oklahoma Press, 1982).

83. Paul Hutton, "Why is This Man Forgotten?" *True West* (March 2006), 24–32.

84. Marley Shebala, "Fort Defiance Wants No Reminders of Kit Carson," *The Navajo Times* 19 January 2006, A–3.

85. Jose Cisneros and Gregory Scott Smith, "The Bosque Redondo Memorial: Long Deserved, Long Overdue," *El Palacio* vol. 108, no. 4 (Winter 2003): 14–18.

Bibliography

American Indian and Alaska Native Population 2000. Washington, D.C. U.S. Census Bureau. 2002. Available online at *www.census .gov/prod/2002pubs/c2br01-15pdf.*

Bailey, Lynn R. *Bosque Redondo: The Navajo Internment at Fort Sumner, New Mexico, 1863–68.* Tucson, Ariz.: Westernlore Press, 1998.

Begay, Richard. "Tsé Bíyah 'Anii'ahí: Chaco Canyon and Its Place in Navajo History." In David Grants Nobel, ed., *In Search of Chaco: New Approaches to an Archaeological Enigma.* Santa Fe, N.M.: School of American Research Press, 2004.

Bighorse, Tiana. Edited by Noel Bennett. *Bighorse the Warrior.* Tucson, Ariz.: University of Arizona Press, 1990.

Brooks, James F. *Captives and Cousins: Slavery, Kinship and Community in the Southwest Borderlands.* Chapel Hill: University of North Carolina Press, 2002.

———. "This Evil Extends Especially to the Feminine Sex: Captivity and Identity in New Mexico, 1700–1846." In Elizabeth Jameson and Susan Armitage, eds. *Writing the Range: Race, Class, and Culture in the Women's West.* Norman: University of Oklahoma Press, 1997.

Brugge, David M. "Navajo Prehistory and History to 1850." In Alfonso Ortiz ed., *Handbook of the North American Indians: Southwest 10* Washington, D.C.: Smithsonian Press, 1983.

———. Navajos in the Catholic Church Records of New Mexico, 1694–1875. Tsaile, Ariz.: Navajo Community College Press, 1985.

———, trans. "Vizcarra's Navajo Campaign of 1823." *Arizona and the West: A Quarterly Journal of History* 6, no. 3 (autumn 1964): 223–44.

Correll, J. Lee. *Through White Men's Eyes: A Contribution to Navajo History* Vol. 2. Window Rock, Ariz.: Navajo Heritage Center, 1979.

Denetdale, Jennifer Nez. *Reclaiming Diné History: The Legacies of Navajo Chief Manuelito and Juanita*. Tucson: University of Arizona Press, 2007.

Faris, James C. *Navajo and Photography: A Critical History of the Representation of an American People*. Albuquerque: University of New Mexico Press, 1996.

Gregg, Josiah. *Commerce of the Prairies*, 2 vols. 1844. Reprint, Ann Arbor, Mich.: University Microfilms, 1966.

Hoffman, Virginia, and Broderick H. Johnson. *Navajo Biographies*, vol. 1. Phoenix, Ariz.: Navajo Curriculum Center Press, 1974.

Hutton, Paul. "Why is This Man Forgotten?" *True West*. March 2006.

Iverson, Peter. *The Navajo Nation*. Albuquerque: The University of New Mexico Press, 1981.

———. *Diné: A History of the Navajos*. Albuquerque: University of New Mexico Press, 2002.

Jim, Rex Lee. "A Moment in My Life." In Arnold Krupat and Brian Swann, eds. *Here First: Autobiographical Essays by Native American Writers*. New York: Modern Library, 2000.

Johnson, Broderick H., ed. *Navajo Stories of the Long Walk Period*. Tsaile, Ariz.: Navajo Community College Press, 1973.

Kelley, Klara B., and Harris Francis. "Abalone Shell Buffalo People: Navajo Narrated Routes and Pre-Columbian Archaeological Sites." *New Mexico Historical Review* 78, no. 1 (winter 2003): 29–58.

Kelly, Lawrence. *Navajo Roundup: Selected Correspondence of Kit Carson's Expedition Against the Navajo, 1863–1865*. Boulder, Colo.: Pruett, 1970.

Keleher. William A. *Turmoil in New Mexico, 1846–1868*. Santa Fe: The Rydal Press, 1952.

Lavender, David. *The Southwest*. New York: Harper and Row, 1980.

———, ed. *The Navajo Treaty—1868: Treaty between the United States of America and the Navajo Tribe of Indians/With a Record of the Discussions that Led to Its Signing*. Las Vegas, Nev.: K.C. Publications, 1968.

Link, Martin, ed. Navajo: 1868: *A Century of Progress*. Window Rock, Ariz.: KC Publications and the Navajo Tribe, 1968.

———. *The Navajo Treaty—1868: Treaty Between the United States of America & the Navajo Tribe of Indians/With a Record of Discussions That Led to Its Signing*. Las Vegas, Nevada: KC Publications, 1968.

Locke, Raymond Friday. *The Book of the Navajo*. Los Angeles: Mankind Press, 1992.

M'Closkey, Kathy. *Swept Under the Rug: The Hidden History of Navajo Weaving*. University of Arizona Southwest Center Series. Albuquerque: University of New Mexico Press, 2002.

McCullough-Brabson, Ellen and Marilyn Help. *We'll Be in Your Mountains, We'll Be in Your Songs: A Navajo Woman Sings*. Albuquerque: University of New Mexico Press, 2001.

McNitt, Frank. *Navajo Wars: Military Campaigns, Slave Raids and Reprisals*. Albuquerque: University of New Mexico Press, 1990.

Roessel, Robert A. *A Pictorial History of the Navajo from 1860 to 1910*. Rough Rock, Ariz: Navajo Curriculum Center, Rough Rock Demonstration School, 1980.

Roessel, Ruth. *Women in Navajo Society*. Rough Rock, Ariz.: Navajo Resource Center, 1981.

Shebala, Marley. "Fort Defiance Wants No Reminders of Kit Carson," *The Navajo Times*. January 19, 2006.

Smith, Andrea. *Conquest: Sexual Violence and American Indian Genocide*. Cambridge, Mass.: South End Press, 2005.

Tapahonso, Luci. *Blue Horses Rush In: Poems and Stories*. Tucson: University of Arizona Press, 1997.

Thompson, Fritz and Loie Fecteau, "Kit Carson: Hero or Villain?" *Albuquerque Journal*. March 3, 2002.

Thompson, Gerald. *The Army and the Navajo*. Tucson: University of Arizona Press, 1976.

Towner, Ronald. *Defending the Dinétah: Pueblitos in the Ancestral Navajo Heartland*. Salt Lake City: University of Utah Press, 2003.

Trafzer, Clifford E. *Anglo Expansionists and Navajo Raiders: A Conflict of Interest*. Historical Monograph No. 3. Tsaile, Ariz.: Navajo Community College Press, 1978.

————. *The Kit Carson Campaign: The Last Great Navajo War*. Norman: University of Oklahoma Press, 1982.

Utter, Jack. "The Death of a Navajo Patriot—And His Ties to Federal Recognition, Treaty Rights, the Trust Relationship, and the San Juan Water Settlement." Unpublished paper in author's possession, August 3, 2004.

White, Richard. *The Roots of Dependency: subsistence, Environment, and Social Change Among the Choctaws, Pawnees, and Navajos*. Lincoln: University of Nebraska Press, 1983: 212–290.

Wilkins, David E. *The Navajo Political Experience*. Tsaile, Ariz.: Diné College Press, 1999.

Willink, Roseann Sandoval, and Paul Zolbrod. *Weaving a World: Textiles and the Navajo Way of Seeing*. Santa Fe: Museum of New Mexico Press, 1996.

Yazzie, Ethelou. *Navajo History*. Chinle, Ariz.: Navajo Curriculum Center, Rough Rock Demonstration School, 1971.

Young, Robert. *The Role of the Navajo in the Southwest Drama*. Gallup, N.M.: Gallup Independent and the Navajo Tribune, 1968.

Zolbrod, Paul. *Diné Bahane': The Navajo Creation Story*. Albuquerque: University of New Mexico Press, 1984.

CD RECORDINGS

Begay, Jay, and Everitt White. *The Long Walk—Hwééldi*. Canyon Records, 1999.

Cody, Radmilla. "The Return Home." *Song in Seeds of Life: Traditional Songs of the Navajo*. Phoenix, Ariz.: Canyon Records, 2001.

Primeaux, Verdell, and Johnny Mike, "Blood, Sweat and Tears." In *Hours Before Dawn: Harmonized Peyote Songs of the Navajo American Church*. Phoenix, Ariz.: Canyon Records, 2002.

Further Reading

Bailey, Lynn R. Bosque Redondo: The Navajo Internment at Fort Sumner, New Mexico, 1863–68. Tucson, Ariz.: Westernlore Press, 1998.

Bighorse, Tiana. Edited by Noel Bennett. *Bighorse the Warrior*. Tucson, Ariz.: University of Arizona Press, 1990.

Broderick, J. & Roessel, R., eds. *Navajo Stories of the Long Walk Period*. Tsaile, Ariz.: Navajo Community College Press, 1973.

Iverson, Peter. *The Navajo* (Heritage Edition). Philadelphia, Pa.: Chelsea House Publishers, 2005.

——. *Diné: A History of the Navajos*. Albuquerque: University of New Mexico Press, 2002.

Trafzer, Clifford E. *The Kit Carson Campaign: The Last Great Navajo War*. Norman: University of Oklahoma Press, 1990.

WEB SITES

The Navajo
http://www.lapahie.com/

Official Web site of the Navajo Nation
http://www.navajo.org/

The Navajo Nation's Own "Trail of Tears"
http://www.npr.org/templates/story/story.php?storyId=4703136

History and Information on the Navajo
http://southwest.library.arizona.edu/hav7/body.1_div.3.html

Picture Credits

Index

About the Contributors

Author **JENNIFER NEZ DENETDALE** is Diné of the Navajo Nation and of the Tłʼógi [Zia] and ʼAshiih [Salt] clans. Originally from Tohatchi, New Mexico, she earned her Ph.D. in history from Northern Arizona University in 1999. Her research interests include Southwest Native American and Navajo history. Her book, *Reclaiming Diné History: The Legacies of Navajo Chief Manuelito and Juanita,* was published by the University of Arizona Press. She has published articles in *American Indian Culture and Research Journal, Journal of Social Archaeology* and *New Mexico Historical Review* and *Wicazo Sa Review.*

Series editor **PAUL C. ROSIER** received his Ph.D. in American History from the University of Rochester in 1998. He currently serves as assistant professor of history at Villanova University, where he teaches Native American history, the environmental history of America, history of American Capitalism, and world history. Dr. Rosier is the author of *Rebirth of the Blackfeet Nation, 1912–1954* (2001) and *Native American Issues* (2003). His next book, on post–World War II Native American politics, will be published in 2008 by Harvard University Press. Dr. Rosier's work has appeared in various journals, including the *Journal of American History*, the *American Indian Culture and Research Journal*, and the *Journal of American Ethnic History.*